CULTURALLY
RESPONSIVE
SCHOOL LEADERSHIP

SERIES | **RACE** AND
EDUCATION

Series edited by H. Richard Milner IV

CULTURALLY RESPONSIVE SCHOOL LEADERSHIP

MUHAMMAD KHALIFA

HARVARD EDUCATION PRESS
CAMBRIDGE, MASSACHUSETTS

Fifth Printing, 2020

Paperback ISBN 978-1-68253-207-2
Library Edition ISBN 978-1-68253-208-9

Library of Congress Cataloging-in-Publication Data
Names: Khalifa, Muhammad A., 1975– author.
Title: Culturally responsive school leadership / Muhammad Khalifa.
Other titles: Race and education series.
Description: Cambridge, Massachusetts : Harvard Education Press, 2018. |
    Series: Race and education series | Includes bibliographical references and index.
Identifiers: LCCN 2018012888| ISBN 9781682532072 (pbk.) |
    ISBN 9781682532089 (library edition)
Subjects: LCSH: Educational equalization—United States. | Educational
    leadership—United States. | Discrimination in education—United States. |
    Multicultural education—United States. | Minority students—United States. |
    Critical pedagogy.
Classification: LCC LC213 .K448 2018 | DDC 371.2—dc23
    LC record available at https://lccn.loc.gov/2018012888

Published by Harvard Education Press,
an imprint of the Harvard Education Publishing Group

Harvard Education Press
8 Story Street
Cambridge, MA 02138

Cover Design: Wilcox Design
Cover Photo: Blend Images – Hill Street Studio/Brand X Pictures/Getty Images
The typefaces used in this book are Adobe Garamond Pro, Milo OT, and Proxima Nova.

CONTENTS

SERIES FOREWORD

H. Richard Milner IV
Race and Education Series Editor

A much-needed addition to the literature on equity and leadership, Muhammad Khalifa's volume is one of the first to outline tenets of culturally responsive leadership, and demonstrate how school leaders can implement these powerful principles and practices in their schools. Focusing on one urban school populated by students who have been "failed" by traditional educational structures and systems, the volume showcases a range of culturally responsive leadership pedagogical tools that may be crafted—and adapted—to align with students' and parents' needs across educational, social and cultural settings. To assist leaders in designing more inclusive educational environments that promote school and life success, Khalifa argues that culturally responsive leadership must focus explicitly on race, as well as account for local traditions and Indigenous cultures to support students.

A central goal of the Race and Education series is to advance a critical, forward-thinking body of research on race that contributes to policy, theory, practice, and action. Although the series will advance scholarship in race studies, a central objective is to assist educators—real teachers, school counselors, administrators, coaches, and outside-of-school providers—in their efforts to center the very humanity of students whose needs are far from being understood, responded to, and met in schools and in society.

Several interrelated objectives guide the series:

- to study race and develop explicit recommendations for eliminating racism, discrimination, and other forms of oppression from educational efforts and institutions
- to address race by means of multidisciplinary expertise and approaches
- to examine various layers of inequity through micro-, meso-, and macrolevel lenses that will expose individual and systemic barriers that prevent equitable opportunities for students of color
- to explore the many assets and strengths of students, communities, and families, thereby challenging inaccurate narratives, policies, and practices which suggest that students of color need "fixing," and instead reinforcing how students of color succeed when mechanisms are in place to support them
- to advance scholarly attention to aspects of racism and discrimination while also (and most importantly) offering real, action-driven assistance to educators and others who work with and on behalf of students of color inside and outside of schools as institutions

Grounded in and substantiated by empirical research, the series aims to highlight action designed to help solve problems of race in education. In this sense, it will look to address both societal issues and educational practices. The books included in the series will be developed to highlight scholarship from leading researchers in the field as well as emerging scholars and will investigate mechanisms, systems, structures and practices that have a real bearing on students' opportunities to learn.

Racial justice is arguably the most important educational imperative of our time. Considering the inextricable links between society and education, educators have the potential to help equip students with knowledge, tools, attitudes, dispositions, mind-sets, beliefs, and practices to create a world that is truly equitable for its citizenry. Series titles will attend to issues both inside and outside of schools, shedding light on what matters and how we, in education, can improve practices that systemically improve the life chances of students.

Above all, the Race and Education series asks the important question, *Do we have the fortitude to center race in our work, or will we continue going about our business, our work, as usual?* I am always mindful of curriculum theorist Beverly Gordon's provocative observation that "critiquing your own assumptions about the world—especially if you believe the world works for you"—is an arduous endeavor.[1] At the very heart of this series is an explicit challenge to those in power to work for the good of humanity, to interrupt systems, policies, and practices that work only for some while others remain underserved. It asks: How do the effects of poverty and compromised opportunities in transportation, housing, and employment manifest themselves in how communities respond to social (in)justice? What role does and should education play in understanding and responding to these manifestations? What roles do teachers play in helping students develop insights about the salience of race in society? How do education policy makers respond to these realities when making decisions about what gets covered in the curriculum? The books in this series will address many of these questions about race, racism, and discrimination to advance what we know in education and to move us toward a more equitable education system.

Indeed, a primary premise of the series is that we must learn from a diverse range of disciplines to build and sustain efforts on behalf of students who continue to be underserved in education. Thus, scholars from a variety of disciplines—sociology, psychology, health sciences, political science, legal studies, and social work—can assist us in reversing trends in education that continue to have devastating effects on student experiences and outcomes. What is clear from solid evidence is that these students succeed when appropriate mechanisms are in place. The Race and Education series will contribute to this tradition, centralizing those mechanisms that will help us reach our true ideal democracy. I am ready. I am hopeful that readers of the series are as well.

Welcome! #LetsDotheWork!

FOREWORD

This book unexpectedly brought me back to a much earlier time in my career, to a place far removed from the urban Michigan school detailed within its pages. I was a young education professor based in Fairbanks, visiting schools in isolated rural villages in the vast expanses of Alaska. Each school served one small village of a few hundred Native Alaskan residents, with a K–12 population of about sixty or fewer students. The teachers at most schools were white, from "the Lower 48," as were the principals. In each village, the school staff were typically housed in a compound separate from the village residents, and seldom participated in the daily life of the students and their community.

Little of the students' vibrant cultural life was reflected in the schools—not the people they encountered, the curriculum they studied, the interactional patterns they experienced, or even the language they were expected to speak. Not only were the school staff not versed in the children's culture, but they also saw the students' culture as problematic to their success in school.

Once when a principal was talking to me about his school's poor academic performance, his explanations centered around his struggle to help the teachers learn to keep the students on the right path, especially when they went back to homes that undid everything the school was trying to accomplish. Originally from a state far from rural Alaska, he likened himself to a military general working in a foreign land. Suddenly, it all made sense to me. He was the general, the teachers were the officers, the students were the troops in training . . . and the community? The community was the enemy.

I think most observers would intuitively realize that an institution that fashioned itself as the enemy of one's community, one's family, and all that one holds dear could not successfully peddle its academic wares to those who were unwillingly drafted into its confines for seven hours a day, five days a week. And yet, the non–Alaska Native principals and teachers continued to assert that the reason the children weren't learning had nothing to do with what the educators were or were not doing, but could be completely explained by the fact that the *communities* did not support the *schools*.

While it's perhaps not as starkly obvious as in rural Alaska, I have regularly encountered the same perspective in many urban schools in the mainland United States. The schools, the teachers, and the principals say that the children are unmotivated; that no matter what the educators do in schools, the children return to dysfunctional, uncaring, crime-ridden, single-parent homes and communities. In other words, the troops cannot be trained properly because they insist on fraternizing with the enemy.

This volume offers a completely different paradigm. What if educational leaders could learn to embrace students' lived realities as part of their schooling, rather than insist that to succeed in school they must abandon everything that has nurtured and supported them thus far in their life journeys? What if the school could not only embrace the community, but seek to work with students, parents, and others to make use of community resources for instructional purposes, and design school curricula to collectively address long-standing community problems? What if the school, the students, and the community were on the same side?

If we are to convince more students in our country's urban schools to embrace the education offered at these institutions, then we have to help school leaders learn to stop blaming the students and the communities, and start changing the institutions. This book, through an ethnographic study of one school and one enlightened, self-reflective school leader, Joe, provides a road map to accomplish that goal. Within its pages, school leaders can learn to break through the confines of their traditional principal training paradigms, and leap into a brave new world of providing real education for *all* students. They can learn how to develop culturally responsive teachers and instruction; create physically and emotionally safe spaces for students who have been treated poorly in school settings; fight racist, sexist, xenophobic, and homophobic policies; and connect with parents and communities in new and mutually beneficial ways. The success of our urban schools depends on how quickly that knowledge can be made available to and adopted by a much wider audience.

It's time.

Lisa Delpit
Felton G. Clark Distinguished Professor of Education
Southern University and A&M College

INTRODUCTION

Leaders who do not act dialogically, but insist on imposing their decisions, do not organize the people—they manipulate them. They do not liberate, nor are they liberated: they oppress.

—PAULO FREIRE, *Pedagogy of the Oppressed*

For the past twenty years, I have worked closely with school leaders. I have done so as a public school teacher, a lead teacher, a central district administrator, and as a professor who trained leaders and conducted research about school leadership. Though my experiences have been diverse, I open this book where my experiences as an educator began—as a middle school science teacher on the East Side of Detroit. It was a fascinating, dynamic experience for my students and for me. I felt love, rage, care, grief, hostility, and even despair in my experiences with mainly Black students and families, as well as Albanians, poor Polish and other Whites who couldn't afford to leave the city, Somalis, Bengali, Yemeni, and recently immigrated Levantine Arabs. Unfortunately, early on, I was socialized into accepting deficit-based understandings about many of these poor and minoritized students. I had little knowledge of the contexts of oppression that my students faced, which included deindustrialization, illicit drug encroachment in their space, mass incarceration, federally sponsored destruction of Black economic centers (such as the "urban renewal" of Black Bottom and Paradise Valley), and even refugee camps and forced migration. Therefore, through my own ignorance, it was easy for me to accept the deficit narratives that my more experienced mentor colleagues passed my way.

When they said to me, for example, that parents "don't show up to school because they don't care about their kids' education," I entertained the unfair "deficit" depiction of the families because only a few showed up for parent-teacher conferences. When colleagues characterized parents as "aggressive" or "apathetic," I swallowed that poison as well. For, when parents did come in, they seemed to be on edge, aggressive, or even oppositional and angry; it was, again, easy for me to accept my colleagues' explanation that "students cut up in class because, well, look at the parents' anger. Look at where they learned it from." So there I was, myself an educated Black man from a socially conscious Black "protest" family, *deciding* to teach in Detroit to help impoverished Black students, and I was guilty as charged: I held and espoused deficit-oriented constructions of Black (and other minoritized) students and I pathologized segments of our communities. Despite my professed love for them, I was complicit in the oppression of my own students and communities of color.

CONTEXT OF DAVISTOWN'S MINORITIZED URBAN YOUTH

I understood some of the daily challenges my students faced, but not much about the historical policies and practices that led to those challenges. I did not yet understand that the curriculum and pedagogy, school structures, programs and activities, and other aspects of schooling were not designed for them. I only later came to realize that all students need culturally responsive leadership and schooling; but minoritized students hardly ever have access to it.[1] This work follows the educational experiences of minoritized students—those who have been historically marginalized in school and society. In this book, I suggest that school leaders can promote schooling that addresses the unique learning *and cultural* needs of students who are Indigenous, Black, Latinx, low-income, refugees, or otherwise minoritized. Throughout this work, I place three bodies of knowledge into an ongoing conversation: one, I constantly reflect on my own experiences as a public school teacher and administrator; two, I incorporate the extant research and literature available on culturally responsive leadership; and three, I mostly examine data that I have collected in my own research contributions. The research project that I pull from most occurred in Davistown, Michigan (pseudonym)—a midsized, Rust Belt college town—and in a school called Urban Alternative High School (UAHS, a pseudonym).

Primary Research Setting and Methodology

Michigan has some of the most respected teacher training programs in the nation, and has state-level mandates that require equitable schooling. Yet despite well-intentioned educators and policy makers, Black, Brown, and other minoritized students were deeply underserved at the time I was there. In this book I share rich data from the UAHS principal, Joe—an African American school leader who had worked in schools for over forty years. I also explore student experiences by following students in and out of classrooms, throughout the school, and into their homes and communities. During the time of this research, I also lived in one of several predominantly minoritized communities in the Detroit area. While I also include data from other districts in Michigan and from districts around San Antonio, Texas, my research in Greater Detroit is what drives this book.

By examining data from a two-year ethnographic study of UAHS principal Joe, I investigate and theorize about the central role of culturally responsive school leadership in school reform. I employed an array of ethnographic research activities: extensive field notes with dense descriptions; interviews and member checking; analysis of available school, district, and county data; regular visits to school and community-based sites; and an analysis of reports and media that have highlighted the research site. To capture this unique expression of culturally responsive school leadership, I began by visiting the school one or two times per week and increased my presence over time. This approach enabled me to build rapport with those in the school, and as the participants' comfort increased, so did my presence. As the purpose of ethnographic research is to understand the cultural context and discursive statements and actions in the research setting, these research methods allowed me to understand cultural nuances and the relationship between the school and the surrounding community.

Davistown is a short drive from Detroit, which Secretary of Education Arne Duncan referred to in 2011 as the "ground zero of education." There is a long-running tendency of educational reformers and government officials to choose the starkest, most troubling, and most alarming language when discussing minoritized communities, especially Black spaces like Detroit. This is true because of historical understandings of Black people as subhuman, inherently troubled, dangerous when independent or noncompliant, and in need of being either saved or controlled. Detroit has been all of that to Michiganders, and even the nation, as Secretary Duncan demonstrated.

But his comment left much open for interpretation; was Detroit's educational condition the fault of these Black families, who were in some way deficient, or was it the result of decades of anti-Black sentiment and federal/state policy that eviscerated and strangled Black Detroit? According to historian Thomas Sugrue and other scholars, it was the latter.[2] Detroiters experienced decades of deindustrialization and middle-class job loss, and even when job creation did happen, it was likely in low-wage industries such as retail and restaurants; people could no longer support their families on one—or even two—incomes. As the middle-class automotive jobs moved out of Detroit, first to suburbia or rural areas, and then out of the country, poverty and joblessness steadily took root. Deindustrialization, however, would not be the only systemically oppressive force experienced by poor Black and Latinx Detroiters.

And on a final researcher note: on occasion throughout this text, I recount my positionalities, experiences, biases, feelings, and growth. It has often been stated that ethnography is cultural work, or the work of doing culture. But so many age-old questions complicate this understanding of ethnographic work: Whose culture can be seen? By whom? If it is seen, who can represent it? What is not seen even though we are all looking and experiencing? Who can represent that culture? Why did we want to see that culture in the first place? And are we contributing to oppression of these cultures by potentially exoticizing them to cultural outsiders? I have no good answer for most of these questions, and in this book, I do not take them up. But I am sensitive to and reflect on such questions throughout the text.

But it is also the case that ethnography can be painful and disruptive. This is especially true for those doing ethnography around the lives of oppressed and marginalized peoples. It is painful because you can often do little to stop the oppression; it is painful when you are asked to help, but are not in a position to do so; it is painful when you know that much of the minoritization you see will be reproduced. And it is painful when we, as researchers, swing heavily (and stay) into a "space of critique." I hold the position that it is useful for some of us scholars to issue ongoing critiques; and likewise, that it is useful for some of us to use the critique to move into culturally responsive practices to improve the lives of students in school. This all speaks to the process of ethnography, the impact it has on the researcher, and the disruption it can have for the participants in the study.

Yet, I find solace in some of the transformations that I witnessed in this study. For many years, the conversations around "outcomes" or "results" tended to focus on test score data of minoritized students. In more recent years, others have pushed back against such a narrow focus on test scores, and have argued that measures such as classroom grades and academic progress over the year should also be considered when evaluating the progress of districts. In each chapter of this book, I share descriptions of the outcomes of this study, and every one is different for each of the content chapters (chapters 2–5). Chapter 2 indicates one of the possible results of critically self-reflective leadership: how the various stakeholders begin to question their personal and organizational roles in oppression. This, in turn, enables students and families to see leaders as fair. The typical suspicion that some minoritized students have toward school was not present, and they (UAHS students) *would* be able to learn from them (UAHS teachers).

In chapter 3, the data provides details of how minoritized students can be in school and not feel marginalized or criminalized. So the "outcomes" of CRSL in this chapter demonstrate how the children expressed that they felt a sense of belonging in school. In chapter 4, I affirm how student identities associated with minoritized communities were accepted in school, and in particular how these identities were humanized and honored despite the coterminous promotion of academic student identities in school. The result was that students expressed both comfort and a sense of belonging in school, despite their historical feelings of marginalization in school. Another outcome of this process of teachers' willingness to honor multiple student identities was that students, even while retaining their Indigenous identities, began to craft long-term academic goals for themselves—something they had not previously done. The final chapter in which I report outcomes is chapter 5, wherein I describe ways that school leaders promote culturally responsive curriculum and instruction. The results in this chapter are reported out in a couple of different ways—first, in the ways that teachers say they can relate their classroom pedagogies to students' lives, and second, in how students now say they enjoy and can identify with the content in and out of UAHS classrooms. I report in the final chapter that this all led to a model of schooling that was honored and, to an extent, even led with community (histories, experiences, perceptions) at its core.

Is Oppression Automatically Reproduced?

For culturally responsive school leaders, it is absolutely necessary to understand contexts and histories of the students and their communities. Oppressive structures and practices in schools will remain in place unless (a) the status quo is challenged and (b) educators and leaders know *how* to properly push against oppression. In Detroit, the types of oppression were so ubiquitous and diverse that it is really hard to assess the depth of the impact; from the late 1800s until the late 1900s, these included racially oppressive occupational, housing, educational, and judicial policies. Thus, in addition to deindustrialization, practices like police brutality, urban disinvestment, and highway expansion onto Black economic areas all devastated Black areas of the city. But what would later happen to Black communities would make deindustrialization and these earlier forms of oppression seem smaller in scale. The federally supported policies in the 1980s and later that contributed to the influx of crack cocaine would come to decimate minoritized (particularly Black and Latinx) communities in ways not witnessed since Reconstruction; in particular, an explosion in the incarceration rates—and the permanent stigma that ex-convicts would bear.

But unlike slavery, Black lynching, and Jim Crow policies—where anti-Black oppression was still justified by but embarrassing for Whites—now these Blacks were understood to be deserving of the oppression they faced because of their own behaviors. Or worse, they were blamed for creating their own oppressive structures: they were imprisoned because they broke laws; their schools were under-resourced because they mismanaged money; the jobs left the city because it was unsafe due to Black crime; and the murder rate was so high because unruly Blacks were killing themselves. The prison-industrial complex emerged from this context, which was a policy of containment of subhuman minorities consistent with earlier dispossession of Indigenous native lands, Native American schools, chattel slavery, Jim Crow policy, racialized policing practices, mass incarceration, and racial housing policy, among other historical oppressive practices.

The role of federal and state policy in producing these outcomes for Black communities is rarely discussed. That the CIA facilitated the entrance and distribution of massive amounts of crack cocaine and heroin into Black and Latinx communities to quell the rage and protest exemplified by oppressed Blacks across the United States was not considered.[3] Yet, many state and federal policies led to high crime and poverty rates. Racist housing policies and high residential mobility within minoritized communities, oppression and liminalizing of Indigenous space/bodies, deindustrialization, drug addiction, violent crime, and the prison-industrial complex all permanently changed minoritized communities. The personal experiences that have followed such policies have been devastating for many minoritized families. For example, I personally know seventeen boys and men—all Black males, including four cousins—who were murdered in Southeast Michigan; it is mind-boggling that literally hundreds of thousands of other Black and Latinx men have been murdered since the mid-1980s. Such discussions must be brought into schools as you begin to learn what it means to be a culturally responsive school leader.

Connecting Context to School Leadership

What exactly does any of this context have to do with education or school leadership? Communities have collective histories, experiences, and memories, and therefore have a unique way of viewing the world, and school. When my teacher colleagues in Detroit offered deficit descriptions of students and communities, I was egregiously unaware of any of the historical processes that constructed the communities in which their children lived. Unfortunately, such uninformed views not only allowed us to blame Black families for failing schools and community underdevelopment, but also signaled a lack of historical awareness of the communities served—something necessary for culturally responsive schooling. Most frightening, though, is that it allowed us to dehistoricize the oppression of the community, and therefore to continue the erasure of the community's histories and positionalities in the school. We were blinded to the various ways we contributed to the oppression of the children we claimed to serve. This all suggests that oppression—here, meaning the ways in which students are marginalized in school—will be automatically reproduced unless there are intentional efforts to confront the oppressive structures in society and schooling. Indeed, I acknowledge that there is no single story. Many other minoritized communities also have similar histories of oppression, and even within Detroit, the narratives are many.

LEADERSHIP + COMMUNITY + CULTURE?

Culturally responsive school leaders have a role in the communities they serve. The Western school leadership model in which principals remain in the school and have identities as individual administrators aligned to schools is starkly different from how many minoritized leaders enact school leadership. For example, Murakami and colleagues found that Latinx school principals connected their leadership to the community-based experiences of students and their parents.[4] For Indigenous leaders from Yukon lands in Canada, storytelling is an integral part of school leadership and serves to connect schools and local communities. And Siddle Walker's historical analysis of the relationship between a community and a segregated Black school in the South from 1933 to 1969 suggests that "the parents depended on the school's expertise, guidance, and academic vision, and the school depended on the parents' financial contributions, advocacy, and home-front support."[5] Her historical analysis of early Black schooling challenges current understandings of parental involvement; the parents in her study were involved in the school in culturally specific ways. For example, while parents may not have been engaged in school in ways that many school leaders would recognize, they collectively served as the economic backbone of the school and advocated for causes that improved communities and schools. These historical expressions of Black school-community relationships allow for the following definition of school and community relations: collaborations between school and community stakeholders that benefit school, community, and student performance.

Likewise, according to Morris, early Black principals viewed their "own role as one that extends beyond the boundaries of the school."[6] Both Morris's and Siddle Walker's collective research shows Black principals who were as visible, active, and trusted as other Black community leaders such as pastors, political figures, or organizational heads.[7] These principals also viewed themselves as the "bridge" between themselves and the broader White community and as advocates for *community-based* causes. In her historical analysis, Tillman suggests that "the Black principal represented the Black community; [and] was regarded as the authority on educational, social and economic issues."[8]

Can Principals Be Community Leaders?

When addressing the question of *how* school leaders become community leaders, historical analyses suggest that for early Black principals, *advocating for community causes* was integral to community leadership. This entailed becoming heavily involved not only in school-based priorities, but also in community causes such as civil rights issues. According to Gold and colleagues, contemporary principal advocacy and organizing can actually lead to substantive and sustainable school reform.[9] Therefore, consideration of *principal advocacy* allows us to unpack the ways in which school leaders can include community issues (as opposed to merely school issues) as part of school-community relationships.

WHAT IS EPISTEMOLOGY AND WHY IS IT IMPORTANT?

I argue throughout this book that culturally responsive school principals must lead schools with community perspectives at the center of their leadership behaviors. But how can principals shift from schoolcentric approaches to ones that are in the best interest of the communities they serve? To answer this question, I engage in a brief discussion of *epistemology* and reflect on its relevance for schools. Though the concept of epistemology originated within a branch of philosophy concerned with how knowledge comes to be understood, it has been widely appropriated by education scholars. Epistemology is concerned with anything that informs or influences us in how we learn and understand what we believe is real. For educators engaged in antibias work, this is deeply important. This is partly why people can have different realities for the same topic or phenomenon. One person's (or group's) truth is often not truth for others. Individuals and groups have different histories, experiences, and perceptions, and therefore differ greatly in how they come to know and understand reality; and because of deep epistemological differences between communities, it is difficult to generalize concepts of beauty, appropriateness, importance, or even goodness. Likewise, for educators, understandings of good or aggressive behaviors, disengagement, disrespect, grit, and even achievement are subjective and how parents, students, or community members might understand them can differ vastly. For example, educators and parents might hear the same story about a student, but have different understandings and beliefs of not only what happened, but why it happened. School leaders have always had the power to normalize schoolcentric and educator epistemologies in schools, and to devalue and ignore community-based and Indigenous epistemologies.

Epistemological differences help explain differences that communities have with schoolcentric thoughts of schooling. Cooper, Riehl, and Hasan state, "For the most part, however, traditional notions of parent-school relations have been unidirectional, focused on what is best for the school and children's learning in school and on how parents can assist."[10] Indeed, while "communities" are neither static nor monolithic, and wide differences exist between communities, issues like safety, job growth, immigration and deportation, food security, social justice, and police brutality are likely to be more important issues for minoritized communities than standardized test scores.

In other words, what Cooper, Riehl, and Hasan are questioning is the power of the schoolcentric voice and perspective. Educators have had sole discretion to decide what is acceptable behavior and good learning in schools. Even principals who come from communities in which they work may have schoolcentric epistemologies that do not represent those of the parents and community members. Parents and community people must be fully present—both physically present, and in positions of power and policy making. But again, how can principals do this without colonizing or appropriating community and parent perspectives? It is common to see local school councils, parent-principal partnerships, and other school-community-based partnerships that veer back toward school-based goals; but now they claim to be focusing on math or reading scores, with community voice at the center of the decision to focus on academic gains. Throughout this book, I demonstrate how culturally responsive school leaders engage communities in empowering and humanizing ways, and how they leverage this community engagement to promote school environments in which minoritized students can be successful.

CULTURALLY RESPONSIVE SCHOOL LEADERSHIP

This book is an ethnographic account of how an urban school leader enacted culturally responsive leadership in an alternative school. The research covered in this book offers powerful examples of schooling that will improve the lives of minoritized children who face structural barriers in school and society. I provide a groundbreaking account of how a school leader engaged students, parents, teachers, and neighborhood communities in ways that positively impacted organizational and leadership practice, teacher practice, and student learning. *Culturally Responsive School Leadership* presents three basic premises throughout: (1) that cultural responsiveness is a necessary component of effective school leadership; (2) that if cultural responsiveness is to be present and sustainable in school, it must foremost and consistently be promoted by school leaders; and (3) that culturally responsive school leadership (CRSL) is characterized by a core set of unique leadership behaviors, namely: (a) being critically self-reflective; (b) developing and sustaining culturally responsive teachers and curricula; (c) promoting inclusive, anti-oppressive school contexts; and (d) engaging students' Indigenous (or local neighborhood) community contexts.

Throughout the book, I suggest that leadership in schools should happen in close collaboration with communities, and it should empower children and families; such leadership signals that an equitable power-sharing relationship between communities and schools is optimal. Yet this core goal of empowering children and communities is often overwhelmed by a rigid, traditional top-down approach to education that emphasizes curriculum, testing, compliance, and accountability. Moreover, researchers have found some schools to be subtractive and even oppressive to minoritized students.[11] In the research outlined in this book, the minoritized students were so vigorously pressured in their traditional schools—for behaviors associated with their cultural background and ways of being—many chose to leave school. For example, students were targeted for their tone and manner of speech, clothing, modes of play and competition, cultural proclivities interpreted as aggressive, and many other offenses for which they were more likely to be suspended than their White peers.

Why CRSL? Settler Colonialism, Black Slavery, and Other Types of Oppression

When I enter schools to speak with educators and school leaders, I almost always hear a version of this statement: "We know we have problems! We know achievement gaps exist! We don't want to talk about the problems anymore, we just want to know how to fix them!" To address these widespread sentiments, we must understand something of the origins and nature of US oppression. Why? Because the ways in which Indigenous, Black, Brown, and other minoritized students are currently treated in school is deeply connected with how their bodies, knowledge, land, and communities were constructed at moments in history. Glenn states:

> Settler colonialism should be seen not as an event but as an ongoing structure. The logic, tenets, and identities engendered by settler colonialism persist and continue to shape race, gender, class, and sexual formations into the present . . . settler colonialism's objective is to acquire land so that colonists can settle permanently and form new communities . . . Native inhabitants represent a cheap labor source that can be harnessed to produce goods and extract materials for export to the metropole. They also serve as consumers, expanding the market for goods produced by the metropole and its other colonies. In settler colonialism, the object is to acquire land and to gain control of resources. To realize these ambitions, the first thing that must be done is to eliminate the indigenous occupants of the land. This can be accomplished

in a variety of ways: genocide, forced removal from territories desired by white settlers, and confinement to reservations outside the boundaries of white settlement. It can also be accomplished through assimilation. Assimilation can be biological (e.g., through intermarriage to "dilute" indigenous blood) and/or cultural (e.g., by stripping indigenes of their culture and replacing it with settler culture). The second thing that must be done is to secure the land for settlers. This can be accomplished by imposing a modernist property regime that transforms land and resources (sometimes including people) into "things" that can be owned.[12]

But settler colonialists also invented discourses about minoritized people as they settled lands. Western colonizing nations like the United States have always provided a "story" about why they colonized and vanquished nations and enslaved peoples—claiming, for example, that Indigenous people were exotic subhumans or savages, and they had to be helped by being civilized. This exoticizing, or "othering," is a way of claiming—without explicitly stating—that Whiteness and Westernness is the only way one should exist. This all had deep implications for schooling and education because it is connected to arguments that suggest that schooling should only happen in one particular way. And when Europeans settled and moved to occupy nations and vanquish peoples, they claimed they were helping people who could not improve without European intervention. Schools were used as a point of departure in this regard. Images like the child in figure I.1, from the front cover of *Judge* magazine in 1899, helped sway public opinion and discourse about minoritized people.

While the child being cleaned and civilized by President McKinley appears in the trappings of a Negro and Indigenous American Indian child, he is actually Filipino, with the small caption reading: "The Filipino's First Bath: McKinley—'Oh you dirty boy'!" This picture represents a long tradition of demonizing and savagizing people

FIGURE I.1 "The Filipino's First Bath: McKinley—'Oh you dirty boy!'" in *Judge* magazine (1899).

of conquest—in this case the people of the Philippines, whose colonization had begun one year earlier. As the picture suggests, Americans were civilizing, Christianizing, and cleaning Filipinos of savagery, and this is why America *had* to conquer the land. But to convince the viewers that the Filipinos were subhuman, the artist placed the Filipino child in the image of people that Americans already associated with subhuman savagery—namely Blacks and Indigenous Native Americans.

But how is the exoticizing in this 1899 magazine cover relevant for schooling, and even more so school leadership? Strikingly, when I began teaching Black students in Detroit, both my Black and White colleagues applied modern-day exotic descriptions to our minoritized students. Decolonizing scholars such as Ramon Grosfoguel and Walter Mignolo show how European and American colonizers depicted minoritized peoples as subhuman in multiple ways, but primarily via two distinct paths—biological or cultural. For those who were seen as culturally subhuman, colonizers felt they could easily desavagize them; in the words of Captain Richard H. Pratt, "Kill the Indian, save the man." But for those who were depicted as biologically subhuman, and who had no soul (Grosfoguel), slavery was the only option. Professor William Watkins recalls some of these earlier widespread, subhumanizing biological racist beliefs in his book, *The White Architects of Black Education*:

> White people were characterized by "energetic intelligence," great physical power, stability, inclinations to self-preservation, and a love of life and liberty. Their great weakness, according to Gobineau, was a susceptibility to crossbreeding. Asians were mediocre, lacked physical strength, and wished to live undisturbed. They could never create a viable civilization. Black people, the lowest of all, possessed energy and willpower but were unstable, unconcerned about the preservation of life, given to absolutes, and easily enslaved. . . .
>
> German zoologist Ernst Haeckel, an early advocate of Darwinism, authored *Anthropogenie* in 1874. In this book he situated Blacks on an evolutionary tree below gorillas and chimpanzees. He hypothesized that individuals, in the course of development, relive their evolutionary history, that is, ontogeny recapitulates phylogeny. Building on this theme, race theorists such as D. G. Brinton (1890) argued that some races retained infantile traits rendering them inferior to others (Ehrlich & Feldman, 1977). . . .
>
> For Blacks the pejorative term "oran-outangs" became popular, as it placed them in the realm of chimpanzees and monkeys. Thomas Jefferson used the term "oranootan" in his writings to describe Black men and even himself when he surrendered to his own passions. . . .
>
> In 1799, British surgeon Charles White added a new dimension to the race dialogue. He asserted that Blacks were a separate

species, intermediate between Whites and apes (Tucker, 1994). His book, *An Account of the Regular Gradation in Man and in Different Animals and Vegetables and from the Former to the Latter*, argued that the feet, fingers, toes, legs, hair, cheekbones, skin, arm length, skull size, size of sex organs, and body odor placed Blacks closer to the animal kingdom, most notably apes.[13]

In my work in schools across the United States, contemporary versions of these biological or cultural deficit discourses are often used to describe parents and students. I have heard educator colleagues describe parents as being uncaring or negligent of their children because they do not come to the school for conferences, and blame communities when they feel children misbehave; when students are described as angry, abnormal, irrational, lazy, or even from broken families, and whenever parents and students are blamed for failures of education, I can now trace many of these discourses to earlier forms of racism.

"MINORITIZATION" AS OPPRESSION. Of the hundreds of definitions of oppression in the literature, almost all mention the following terms: *prolonged unjust treatment, control, power,* and *authority.* Some definitions mention words such as *underclass, minority,* and *pressure.* For this book, I would like to focus on systemic understandings of oppression. I embrace these terms and see people in authority as being responsible for enacting or overseeing prolonged unjust treatment of the oppressed. But in my view, oppression is not always intentional and at the forefront of the minds of educators. Oppression is historical, yet its structures continue to shape the lives of minoritized people. It is reproductive, and requires little effort to reproduce. In fact, more effort is needed to *disrupt* oppressive systems found in schools. In this way, it is important to understand that all educators have power in schools, particularly those with leadership responsibilities. When educators enter a school, they will assume control over systems that have been oppressive to students, particularly minoritized students. Educational leaders and teachers will either reproduce oppression, or they will contest it.

Black, Indigenous, Latinx, low-income, LGBTQ, refugee, ELL, and Muslim students are just a few examples of minoritized groups.[14] By placing emphasis on *minoritization*, school leaders call attention to the structural and historical processes that marginalize and oppress group members. Minoritization can happen along racial, ethnic, cultural, linguistic, national, or other lines; the word *minoritize*, as a verb, refers to the ever-morphing nature of how and on whom oppression is enacted. For example, Singh describes the case of *religious* minoritization in the United States: "While there cannot be an official state religion in the United States, Christianity has historically been given unofficial sanction and privilege in virtually every sphere of American life. Resulting from this long tradition of Christian dominance is a strong sense of entitlement and xenophobic entrenchment in significant and powerful sections of the population."[15]

Though the United States is described as a secular nation, Christianity has been given significant privilege in schools. This affects not only how school holiday and vacation breaks are organized, but also the very epistemological, interpretive, and intellectual situating of schools and learning. Thus, in this example, non-Christians are "minoritized" religiously because they face barriers and lack Christian privilege. The same is true across race, gender, class, language, and so on. Even though minoritized students develop agency in school, leaders must still understand the contexts that reproduce systems of oppression and marginalization in school.[16] Without that understanding, it can be difficult to grasp how historically oppressive structures and discourses can continue to minoritize students. In this book I call attention to those structures and discourses that are currently minoritizing students.

A final note about minoritized students: some of my scholar colleagues and friends will undoubtedly question my approach of trying to discuss *all* minoritized students in a single text. They will claim that this dilutes the trove of powerful research that looks deeply at monolithic groups of students, such as Black male, urban youth (in addition to being a Black male myself, this is a group of students on whom I have written extensively). Moreover, how about students who have multiple intersecting identities (e.g., Black *and* low-income *and* ELL *and* refugee without citizenship *and* has been profiled by police)? And what about shifting, dynamic minoritized student identities—for example, those whose parents recently lost jobs, or students who changed their religious status to that of a minoritized group?

There is much validity to such concerns. But I want to be clear here: my choice to discuss minoritized groups together, as a collective, was intentional and reasoned in a few ways. One, I would argue that although differences in how minoritized students are oppressed and marginalized are definitely unique, there are also similarities; in other words, they are all shamed, decentered, physically removed, and asked to acquiesce to spaces that have not honored them or their cultures. So while Indigenous Native Americans, African Americans, and some Latinx groups are statistically more likely to be policed and removed from school, even White low-income students (and other demographic groups) will experience some minoritization as well. Two, this book is about structures, climates, and school organization and how such contexts are reproduced, as well as school leadership practices that can either confront or confirm these contexts. Thus the focus is not so much on a particular minoritized student identity, but rather on how they all identify and experience the systems in which they exist. And finally, the UAHS students were all minoritized—predominantly Black and low-income, but there were also Latinx, Arabs, Indigenous peoples, Southeast Asians, refugees, ELLs, and LGBTQ, among others. It is also important to note that they all were minoritized because of how they were often treated in schools.

SELF-DETERMINATION AND COMMUNITY EMPOWERMENT. Can leaders be culturally responsive if they do not recognize the aspirations of the communities they serve? Indeed, the historical oppressive treatment of minoritized communities—through enslavement, internment, dispossession of lands, and so forth—would understandably impact the epistemologies of minoritized students and communities. In other words, these histories of oppression are directly linked to how students and parents choose to position themselves in community and school. Because of this history of settler colonialism, scholars emphasize the importance of understanding the need for communities to craft their *own goals* based on *community needs.* This may not be aligned (and often is not) with what schools want from children and families. Thus, given the histories of oppression that some communities have faced, self-determination is primarily concerned with community empowerment.

One goal of *community engagement* is for schools to find culturally responsive ways to connect with communities they serve, but this focus remains schoolcentric. The ultimate goal of *community empowerment*, however, is for communities to become healthy, whole, free from oppression, and positioned to craft and live out their own vision. Both are useful, and will benefit the educational experiences of minoritized youth. While some community-based goals and epistemologies may not seem to explicitly espouse educational goals, the results of this study suggest that healthier communities indeed *will* contribute to smarter and more successful students, trusting and engaged parents, and critically self-reflective teachers.

CONTINUING OPPRESSION IN SCHOOLS: HOW SCHOOLS WERE AND CONTINUE TO BE EXCLUSIONARY

Educators often discuss and ponder why "achievement gaps" not only exist but stubbornly persist. Many educators believe their Indigenous American Indian, Latinx, African American, refugee, low-income, and ELL students are generally performing worse than their White middle- and upper-income students. Some districts have invested literally millions of dollars in addressing problems of inequity, going from one reform or consultant to the next, often based on what they have heard other districts were doing. Unfortunately, these reforms have often not worked as well as educators expected; not surprisingly, this has led to reform fatigue. Most schools are evaluated using test scores, class failure rates, and high school graduation rates. Yet few districts have conducted *equity audits* as a way to more precisely implement reforms.[17]

The correlation between school experiences and life opportunities and incarceration has been widely discussed. Scholars have long maintained that school disciplinary experiences are directly connected to prison rates, for instance. Indeed, for many educators, these links are alarming. The figures in the appendix at the end of this chapter, "Data on High School Opportunities and Exclusions," highlight data that is worrisome to most educators.

These figures tell a horrifying story. The earlier graphs demonstrate an incessant racial oppression in US schools that has existed since the beginning of the education of Black, Native American, and Latinx students in the United States. But the later figures (see chapter appendix figures 7, 8, 9, and 10) show the impact of this oppressive education. In other words, the overrepresentation of minoritized students in remedial programs, disabilities programs, disciplinary programs, and poor academic performance directly impacts students' future; it affects their college attendance and graduation rate, their employment rates, and even the likelihood that they will spend time in prison. That is, the same students who are minoritized in education are overrepresented in prison: while Blacks are less that 15 percent of the total US population, they represent 37 percent of the overall inmate population. And Latinx prison rates are not far behind, as their incarceration rate is roughly double their percentage in the general population. But is this correlation between the treatment of minoritized students in school and prison causal? Actually, yes. Many studies are beginning to suggest the two trends are linked.[18]

It is important that educators see that their actions toward minoritized students can, quite literally, impact the life trajectories of those students; it is alarming that educators' treatment of a Black male student, for example, can influence whether or not he ends up in prison! Another telling finding about these figures is the deep connection between academic and disciplinary data. Students who are treated badly in school perform worse, and vice versa. Table I.1 gives

TABLE I.1 Successive oppression

Earlier oppressive practice	Current school practice
Enslaving/confining Blacks on enslavement plantations	Normalizing the practice of sending Black students to in-school suspension spaces
Forcing Native Americans to enroll in "Indian schools" to cleanse them of their Indigenous culture	Preventing Native American students from congregating in a school space
Placing Japanese Americans in internment camps	Allowing students to languish in ESL spaces, even when they are already proficient in English
Lynching Black men, women, and children because of White fears	Cultural or racial shaming of Black students in school
Beating immigrants for speaking native languages in school	Shaming and harassing immigrants for speaking native languages in school

examples of everyday school practices and my attempt to connect them to oppressive historical precedents.

CULTURALLY RESPONSIVE SCHOOL LEADERSHIP, ANTI-OPPRESSION, AND SOCIAL JUSTICE

A commitment to social justice and anti-oppression has become quite important to the field of educational leadership.[19] Though broader in scope, CRSL incorporates aspects of transformative and social justice leadership, mainly critical consciousness and praxis. Cultural responsiveness also focuses on pedagogy, curriculum, and instruction. But for cultural responsiveness to be sustainable, leadership and leadership preparation must be a central part of the conversation. Judith Touré recommends that educational leadership professors and policy makers perform "a reexamination of requirements for leadership preparation which currently lack an emphasis on culturally relevant leadership content knowledge or issues of social justice."[20]

The anti-oppressive stance of school leaders must explicitly include a commitment to advocating for the inclusion of traditionally marginalized students.[21] Madhlangobe and Gordon note that culturally responsive school leaders show determination to create a welcoming school environment for all students and their parents.[22] But this is not easy given that student marginalization is often historical, normalized, and "invisibilized" in most educational contexts. Leaders who are not critically self-aware or knowledgeable about racism and other histories of oppression, and who do not embrace anti-oppression and social justice, will reproduce racism and other forms of systemic oppression in their schools.[23]

The research that I share in *Culturally Responsive School Leadership* raises critical questions about the assumed foundations of educational leadership, as it pushes up against traditional leadership models. While many leadership models focus on instructional and transformational leadership, which almost exclusively highlight the school context, this book draws a broader picture of leadership that centers not on school interests, but on communities. I consider, for example, how neighborhoods and communities have often viewed and interacted with leaders as I explore the current roles of school principals. I begin with an assumption that CRSL behaviors are accessible to *any* school leader truly interested in positive change in her or his school and community.

FOREGROUNDING AND ASSUMPTIONS

This book contributes to emerging scholarship on culturally responsive schooling because, while the overwhelming amount of scholarship has centered on culturally responsive teaching, pedagogy, or curriculum, it has ironically neglected leadership—arguably the most sustaining, salient, and foregrounding aspect of any type of culturally responsive reform. This is an oversight, given that leaders are often considered to be the drivers of reform and the connection between policy and practice. They are also held accountable for the growth and efficacy of their teachers; they are best positioned to improve the practice of teachers who are persistently exclusionary and resistant to cultural responsiveness; they are best poised to develop the willing teachers who can actually *become* culturally unresponsive to new, unfamiliar children; and they are uniquely positioned to impact nonclassroom spaces in the school. I also address the increasingly important topic of how school leaders must become situated in the communities they serve. This book, therefore, focuses on school *leaders* because they have been entrusted to ensure that schools are serving the needs of marginalized children. With this backdrop, I address two broader questions, with a set of subquestions that are addressed in each of the chapters. The broader questions are:

- What are the culturally responsive school leadership behaviors that can improve the lives and educational experiences of minoritized children?
- How can CRSL behaviors be exemplified in other schools?
  The subquestions are:
  - In what ways do schools and school leaders contribute to or resist disparities and inequities in school?
  - What roles do schools and school leaders play in either reproducing or resisting oppression in school environments?
  - How can "traditional" leadership behaviors be adjusted or nuanced to address the needs of minoritized students?
  - What leadership behaviors can support culturally responsive pedagogy, curriculum, and instruction?
  - To what extent must school leaders engage the communities they serve in order to be culturally responsive? What can schools do to earn the trust and credibility of the communities they serve?
  - How can schools validate the identities and aspirations of children they serve?

These questions bring history and theory into focus for practitioners and scholars alike. They allow us to recognize that is not possible to promote culturally responsive schooling without understanding the history of how schools became culturally Eurocentric. The questions also suggest that histories of oppression must be at the center of culturally responsive reforms. There can be no quick fixes or erasures and silencing of historical contexts while promoting equitable schools.

To effectively lead minoritized communities, school leaders must include parents and communities in their leadership activities;

community-based histories and perceptions must be at the center of reform efforts. To push back on education as a schoolcentric enterprise—which recolonizes communities of color in dynamic, iterative ways—school leaders must find ways to engage communities without merely reinscribing schoolcentric perspectives, but with the added claim that schools are "involving" or, even worse, "training" the community. This book puts forth *one* way that this could happen.

ORGANIZATION OF THE BOOK

In chapter 1, I argue that schoolcentric approaches to education oppress and marginalize minoritized students and communities. I theorize about minoritized community oppression and the impact that this oppression has in schools; I explain that some schools and educators are exclusionary not only to students as individuals, but toward entire communities. My primary goal in this chapter is to demonstrate how culturally responsive school leadership positively impacts schools and communities, and how it must be an integral part of any school reform. But the lack of CRSL is a reproduction of oppression, despite the good intentions that some educational leaders may have. The data and narratives in this chapter demonstrate historical tensions between schools and the communities, and trace how and why historical tensions persist between the two. I then trace the historical and cultural aspects of school leadership and school-community partnerships.[24]

Chapter 2 presents the practice of *critical self-reflection* for school leaders who serve minoritized students. Pulling on the works of Gooden and Dantley and Capper, Theoharis, and Sebastian, I present data that suggests that critical self-reflection must be personal, but that it cannot *only* be personal.[25] I look at ways that critical self-reflection must be systemic, and encompass multiple structures throughout schools and districts. Since racism and other types of oppression are so ubiquitous and normalized that they are often invisiblized, the formal and informal school structures must have levers in place that push against oppression. It is inevitable that administrators will either resist, or reproduce and reify, oppression in schools. For this reason, Joe, the principal at UAHS, continually reflected on ways that he and his staff were serving (or underserving) children.

I share evidence of how Joe fostered a staff discourse that placed students' lives at the center of the work at UAHS. This critical self-reflective posture was expressed in different ways; in some instances, Joe coached and mentored staff members, and in other cases, he challenged people directly about their treatment of children. Yet, his work did not stop with the staff; I include descriptions of Joe's administrative practices, such as "rap sessions," that contributed to the *self-advocacy* of students. I conclude the chapter by theorizing about what critical self-reflection and self-advocacy might look like in schools and districts that serve minoritized students.

In chapter 3, I use data to highlight the connection between students, space, and exclusion in school. Using the seminal work of Gupta and Ferguson as well as scholars like Appadurai, Dei, Foucault, and Rosaldo, I show how traditional schools routinely pushed the minoritized students in this study out of school by retrofitting school space to exclusively accommodate middle-class White students.[26] Joe rejected this exclusionary impulse that some of his teachers displayed. Instead, he challenged his teachers to accept many of the behaviors that they personally found distasteful, or even incompliant with school policy and expectations. Joe viewed hip-hop language and aesthetic, as well as "aggressive," "disrespectful," or "insubordinate" behaviors such as sagging pants, marijuana use, and profanity, as subordinate to the students' personal and academic needs. This widening of the school space was a core part of Joe's inclusionary school culture, and this inclusiveness ultimately contributed to student comfort and school completion.

Building on the politics of bodies and space covered in chapter 3, in chapter 4 I present ways that culturally responsive school leaders embrace the expressions of student identity and the voices that are most often marginalized in school. Through a process I call *identity confluence*, the data suggests that students' academic identities are developed alongside local Indigenous identities that typically are pushed out of school. Here the works of Mehan, Hubbard, and Villanueva as well as my own research are both important.[27] This chapter identifies and challenges practices that contribute to the marginalization of minoritized student identities. As the school leader, Joe not only tolerated the local Indigenous and community-based identities, but showed he valued them by engaging and advocating for them. Thus, in addition to refusing to disparage students' Indigenous identities, he promoted a school environment that fostered *academic* identities as well.[28]

Chapter 5 addresses some of the core components of what school leadership is thought to be—instructional leadership of pedagogy and curriculum. Unfortunately, most teachers have not been trained to be culturally responsive educators, and the curricula they use often neglect and are even hostile toward students' cultural knowledge and selves. Many educators have expressed frustration that they do not know *how* to obtain cultural knowledge—either for themselves in improving their craft, or for their curriculum so that their students may see themselves positively represented in the content. In this chapter, I argue that the leader's role is central to developing culturally responsive teachers and curriculum. I use the works of Tillman, Khalifa, Siddle Walker, and Allen, Jacobson, and Lomotey to theorize about the role of principals in developing culturally responsive teachers.[29] This accomplishes another significant development in educational leadership: I use scholarship in an attempt to add culturally responsive lenses to understandings of transformational, distributed, and instructional leadership models.

I draw out my argument in this chapter by sharing ethnographic accounts of how CRSL principals must engage communities in their roles as instructional leaders. Principals are the central driving force of instructional leadership and curriculum development in schools. Extending this case, I share evidence of how Joe developed culturally responsive teachers in his school. I recount how teachers engaged in deal making with students, which is a tactic that lowers academic expectations for minoritized students. Killing students with empathy or kindness, while at the same time requiring little, is—plain and simple—racism, and diminishes students' chances for academic success.[30] But at UAHS, Joe began by modeling and mentoring his teachers out of exclusionary practices. If teachers resisted and remained exclusionary toward students, he worked to more assertively push them toward equity. I use students' connection to and reliance on hip-hop music and aesthetic to demonstrate how principals can help teachers provide a more culturally responsive curriculum. While school leaders certainly have limitations about what can happen within classrooms, this work suggests they can yield considerable pedagogical and curricular influence in schools.

Along with the earlier chapters on school space and student identity confluence, chapter 6 discusses community engagement from the perspective of what most see as school-community relations. Traditional school leaders are often uncomfortable outside of the school walls and a few sporting events. However, the ethnographic findings in this study push the role of the school leader much deeper into the students' home communities. Thus, this paradigmatic shift significantly expands traditional notions of school-community relationships: it not only requires mutual presence of schools and communities, but also engagement in and advocacy for community-based causes. Using my own research as well as the works of other scholars such as Morris, Walker, and Cooper to frame the discussion, I show how principals must venture into communities, though it must be on the community's own terms.[31] I present glimpses of both community-in-school and school-in-community, and conclude the chapter by making the case that CRSL entails an advocacy for community-based causes and interests—which are often unrelated to education or schooling.

I argue that it is not enough to want equity or to have courageous conversations; school leaders must enact school structures that will promote and embrace unique cultural knowledge that is consistent with the lives of children. In this final chapter, I summarize my data and findings and further theorize about the readings covered throughout the book. Cultural responsiveness in schools will never be reached if leaders enact only traditional forms of leadership. Instructional leadership, transformational leadership, curriculum development, and professional development are all important school leadership functions, but they cannot continue to ignore cultural responsiveness.

I end the book with a vignette that brings us back to a concept that predominates in all chapters of the book: community. The setting is the Wilsons' family home, and includes a female student (De'Janae), her mother (April), and grandmother (Helen)—all of whom had been Joe's students at the school. The mother and grandmother attended UAHS because they did not perform well in public schools, and because of their experiences at UAHS, they requested that their daughter be sent to this school as well. The vignette illuminates the presence, trust, rapport, and credibility that this principal (Joe) had with the students he served. I describe how many of the culturally responsive leadership behaviors enacted by Joe in an alternative school can be replicated in any school serving minoritized children.

Throughout his thirty-four-year career at UAHS, Joe successfully fought off several attempts by the district to close the school. His legacy also lives through the community and students he served.

The students began to identify as "smart" and to envision themselves as "going to college"; parents felt that they were contributing to their children's education. And exposed to community-based experiences and knowledge, teachers became critically self-reflective of their own practices, and thus more culturally responsive. In the time since this study was done, Joe has passed away and the school has been closed. This work is dedicated to him, his memory, and his willingness to lead with courage and to share.

APPENDIX TO THE INTRODUCTION

DATA ON HIGH SCHOOL OPPORTUNITIES AND EXCLUSIONS

FIGURE 1 Average NAEP scale scores for grades 4 and 8 in math, 2015

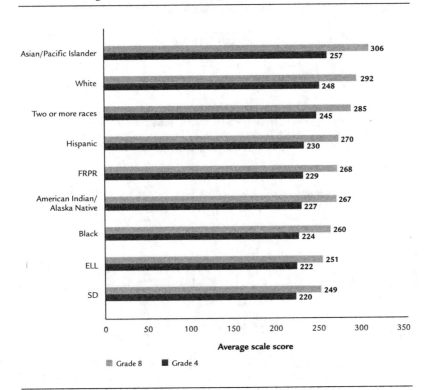

Source: U.S. Department of Education, Institute of Education Sciences, National Center for Education Statistics, National Assessment of Educational Progress (NAEP), 2015 Mathematics Assessment.

Note: FRPR = Free and reduced-price lunch; ELL = English language learners; SD = Students with disabilities

FIGURE 2 Average NAEP scale scores for grades 4 and 8 in reading, 2015

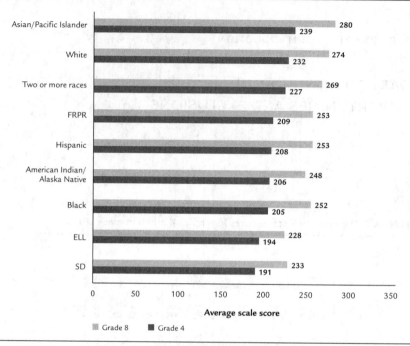

Source: U.S. Department of Education, Institute of Education Sciences, National Center for Education Statistics, National Assessment of Educational Progress (NAEP), 2015 Reading Assessment.

Note: FRPR = Free and reduced-price lunch; ELL = English language learners; SD = Students with disabilities

FIGURE 3 Disciplinary referrals: Percentage of U.S. public school students receiving suspensions (in school and out of school), by race/ethnicity, school year 2011–12

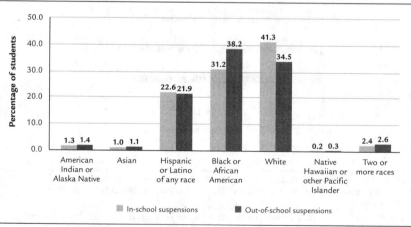

Source: U.S. Department of Education, Office for Civil Rights, Civil Rights Data Collection, 2011–12, available at http://ocrdata.ed.gov. Data notes are available at http://ocrdata.ed.gov/downloads/DataNotes.docx.

FIGURE 4 Student arrest rate: Percentage of U.S. public school students with school-related arrests, by race/ethnicity, school year 2011–12

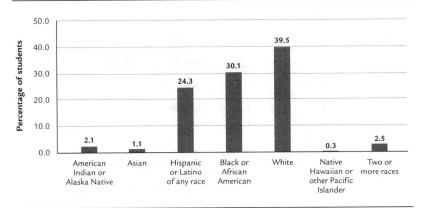

Source: U.S. Department of Education, Office for Civil Rights, Civil Rights Data Collection, 2011–12, available at http://ocrdata.ed.gov. Data notes are available at http://ocrdata.ed.gov /downloads/DataNotes.docx.

FIGURE 5 Gifted and talented enrollment: Percentage of U.S. public school students enrolled in gifted/talented programs, by race/ethnicity, school year 2011–12

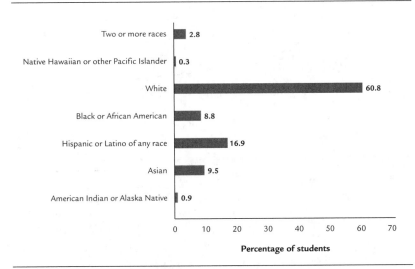

Source: U.S. Department of Education, Office for Civil Rights, Civil Rights Data Collection, 2011–12, available at http://ocrdata.ed.gov. Data notes are available at http://ocrdata.ed.gov /downloads/DataNotes.docx.

FIGURE 6 Students with disabilities: Percentage of U.S. public school students with disabilities served under IDEA, by race/ethnicity, school year 2011–12

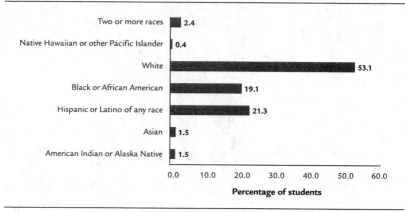

Source: U.S. Department of Education, Office for Civil Rights, Civil Rights Data Collection, 2011–12, available at http://ocrdata.ed.gov. Data notes are available at http://ocrdata.ed.gov /downloads/DataNotes.docx.

FIGURE 7 College attendance: Percentage of students enrolled in degree-granting postsecondary institutions, by year and race/ethnicity, 1976–2014

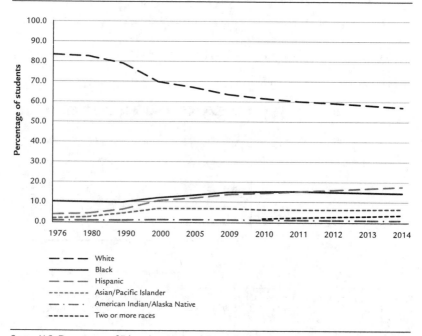

Source: U.S. Department of Education, National Center for Education Statistics, Higher Education General Information Survey (HEGIS), "Fall Enrollment in Colleges and Universities" surveys, 1976 and 1980; Integrated Postsecondary Education Data System (IPEDS), "Fall Enrollment Survey" (IPEDS-EF:90); and IPEDS Spring 2001 through Spring 2015, Fall Enrollment component.

FIGURE 8 Graduation rates: Graduation rates within five years after start from first institution attended for first-time, full-time bachelor's-degree-seeking students at four-year postsecondary institutions, by race/ethnicity, 2008 starting cohort

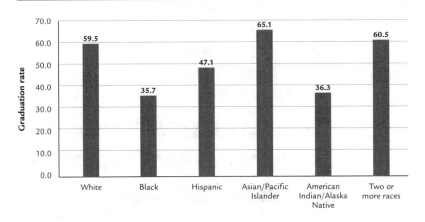

Source: U.S. Department of Education, National Center for Education Statistics, Integrated Postsecondary Education Data System (IPEDS), Fall 2002 and Spring 2007 through Spring 2015, Graduation Rates component; and IPEDS Fall 2008, Institutional Characteristics component. (This table was prepared December 2015.)

FIGURE 9 Unemployment rates: Unemployment rates for persons twenty-five years and over, by race/ethnicity, 2016

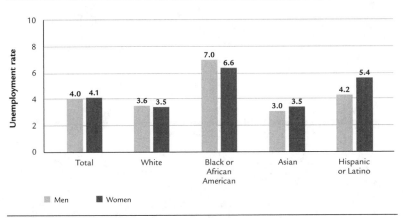

Source: U.S. Department of Labor, Bureau of Labor Statistics, 2016, Table 24, "Unemployed Persons by Marital Status, Race, Hispanic or Latino Ethnicity, Age, and Sex." Available at https://www.bls.gov/cps/tables.htm#charunem.

FIGURE 10 Prison rates: Prisoners under the jurisdiction of federal correctional authorities, by race/ethnicity, December 2015

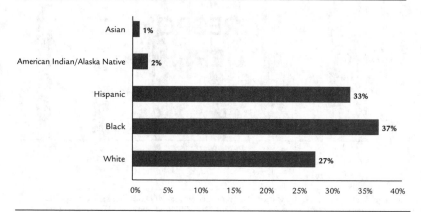

Source: Bureau of Justice Statistics, National Prisoner Statistics, 2015, Appendix Table 3, "Prisoners Under the Jurisdiction of State or Federal Correctional Authorities, by Race and Hispanic Origin," December 31, 2015.

CULTURALLY RESPONSIVE SCHOOL LEADERSHIP

Historical and Community-Based Epistemologies

In order for the settlers to make a place their home, they must destroy and disappear the Indigenous peoples that live there. Indigenous peoples are those who have creation stories, not colonization stories, about how we/they came to be in a particular place—indeed how we/they came to be a place. Our/their relationships to land comprise our/their epistemologies, ontologies, and cosmologies. For the settlers, Indigenous peoples are in the way and, in the destruction of Indigenous peoples, Indigenous communities, and over time and through law and policy, Indigenous peoples' claims to land under settler regimes, land is recast as property and as a resource. Indigenous peoples must be erased, must be made into ghosts.

—EVE TUCK AND WAYNE YANG[1]

Every society needs educated people, but the primary responsibility of educated people is to bring wisdom back into the community and make it available to others so that the lives they are leading make sense.

—VINE DELORIA JR.

In this chapter, I explore why schools continue to be so disconnected from the communities they claim to serve. This disconnect leads schools to be exclusionary places for minoritized children, despite rhetoric around "equitable" or "social justice" education. The questions driving this chapter are the following: Why do parents and students often have completely different interpretations of behaviors and school incidents than teachers and administrators? And why are such differences in interpretation even more stark when the parents and students are Black, Brown, or poor? I also address issues of power. I argue that *community-based* epistemologies and perceptions have often been historically different from (and marginalized by) *school-based*, or schoolcentric, epistemologies. This has posed a long-running, complex problem for schools, and an even bigger problem for students, families, and communities. This is true because school-based epistemologies and interpretations have been normalized in schools, and educators have had exclusive power to define how students and families are characterized and treated in schools. The presence of schools in communities is quite complex because while some students have succeeded by progressing through school and eventually getting a college education, schools have also directly oppressed, or been complicit in the oppression of, communities of color. Finally, perhaps the most compelling question comes back to leadership: How do school leaders either honor and center community-based perspectives in schools, or remain committed to school-based perspectives no matter how marginalizing they are to children and communities?

Historical and cultural aspects of school leadership and school-community partnerships are useful frames in understanding culturally responsive school leadership (CRSL).[2] Scholars argue that school leaders must structure schools in ways that not only accommodate, but also incorporate and celebrate aspects of community. Most schools fail miserably in this regard, and many even act contrarily as they disparage or blame certain communities or cultural behaviors. The data and narratives in this chapter demonstrate historical tensions between schools and minoritized communities, and suggest that culturally responsive school leadership must be integral to any educational reform efforts.

In this chapter, I use a Texas case study to understand how a school and community came to grow far apart. I start with some stark data that should alarm educators and community members alike. I often perform equity audits (found online at ajusted.org) for school districts, which are a practical tool that schools and districts—and parents—can use to identify and address inequities in a school. In addition to looking at federal, state, county, and district data, I administer surveys to as many stakeholders I can find; I ask students, parents, community members, teachers, administrators, cabinet members, and noninstructional employees a host of questions across several "themes" that explain inequity. One thing is clear: educators interpret behavior and education—in fact, the world—very differently from students, parents, and community members. See table 1.1.

While these numbers were taken from an equity audit that I completed in a single school district, they represent a deep divide between school and community that can be witnessed in almost any school or district. In this chapter, I include data from a community in Texas to show how school leaders can make decisions and use language that is culturally unresponsive and disconnected from

TABLE 1.1 Equity audit data sample

	Administrators	Teachers	Parents	Students
Teachers care about students.	97%	98%	39%	21%
Students feel safe at school.	86%	76%	20%	9%
Teachers have a good relationship with parents and members of the community.	93%	45%	13%	9%
There is no difference in how students are treated; they are all treated equally.	76%	94%	10%	3%

Note: Numbers have been rounded to the nearest percentage point.

community epistemology and voice. I then discuss the central role of power, and how schools have wielded this over community voices and perspectives. I look deeply at community-based perspectives and how they have been marginalized in schools.

COMMUNITY-BASED EPISTEMOLOGIES

Often, educators do not understand that minoritized community members who have been historically oppressed see schools differently than teachers, administrators, and other staff. For many community members, schools are "official" institutions; official institutions represent the interests of the local or national government. Schools are viewed within a historical continuum with other official institutions that are also aligned with government. In this chapter, I look deeply at a proposed school closure by a district superintendent in the Greater San Antonio area. It shows just how far apart educator perceptions (based on schoolcentric epistemologies) can be from community-based perceptions.

The Case Study

Due to low enrollment in an oversized building and low academic performance, the superintendent proposed the closure of Frederick Douglass High School (FDHS), which was situated in a historically Black community. The superintendent appointed a committee to make the final determination about closing the school. To reach their decision, committee members were to review statistical indicators such as dropout rate, standardized test scores, enrollment rate, and the cost of running a low-enrollment school. Yet this approach effectively omitted consideration of the central role of race, or any other social, political, or historical factors that might have been considered a part of the decision-making process. When asked about community-based perceptions of the potential school closure, the superintendent (a Latinx male) and the principal (a Black male) refused to engage any of the community-based epistemologies that drove the entire discourse. In the end, thousands of parents and community members rallied together and prevented the closure of the school. District and school administrators and the Black community interpreted the potential closure very differently. In conversations, community members repeatedly interpreted this administrative action (i.e., school closure) within the broader context of how people in the Black community were historically treated.

In other words, racially oppressive issues like redlining, disinvestment of manufacturing jobs in minoritized areas, and economic disinvestment in the Black community—all issues that are not ostensibly related to education—actually all became major factors in how parents viewed schooling. When I arrived in Texas to interview Black parents and community members about the potential closure of FDHS, Black residents explained that the Black community had been long neglected, and had endured systematic forms of racism for the past half-century. Betsy, one Black parent advocate, explained why she thought that anti-Black racism was behind the closure of their "Black school":

> But, continually you see all the development monies being placed, you know, Northside, North East [i.e., White neighborhoods], and maybe some with the manufacturing plant for the Southside [Black neighborhoods] and what not, but continually you can just look at our infrastructure. Just drive over here and drive somewhere else and see what you see. And so we're tired of you know the continual you know neglect and racism, redlining, you know whatever you want to call it over all the years. And so people are going to say, "You're going to take something from us again. You're going to try to take our school."

The parents and community members' discourse could easily be expected, yet it was still unanticipated by the FDHS leaders. The school and district leaders simply could not understand how their interpretations were so different from those of the parents and other community leaders. In their protest, parents relied on community-based epistemologies connected to their own experiences. Their community-based experiences were used as an interpretive lens, heavily rooted in the city's treatment of the Black population.

All of the other perceived racist policies—economic underdevelopment, marginalization of voice, and disregard for interests/views—set the stage for how community members viewed the proposed school closure. One local religious leader on the East Side remarked, "It will kill us economically. Who would buy a home in a neighborhood or area where there's no school? Who would put a business where there are no homes?" This statement suggests that FDHS local residents used community experiences to interpret administrative behaviors, as noted in my earlier research with colleagues.[3] This is not strange, given what Walker and other scholars have narrated about the close connection between parents and community.[4]

During one interview, Betsy also commented, "We believe that if the schools are closed, then our neighborhoods will die." It was unclear whether she was speaking about FDHS or the community in which it was located. Yet district administrators never addressed this confluence of school and community interests. Professor Colleen Larson, in her study of how administrators punished a group of Black students for protesting in school, ultimately found that the "administrators' unwillingness to acknowledge the concerns of the African American community posed a dilemma for the Black community."[5] Despite the fact that district administrators tried to focus the school-closure dialogue on school achievement, enrollment, and finance, community members routinely pointed to community-based factors much broader than the school. For example, a community member during a town hall meeting stated: "Don't close any schools—you will be killing and closing our community."

Unfortunately, the district administrators' actions were not responsive to community epistemologies. For community members, the closure represented the latest iteration of a historical regime of racial marginalization or, essentially, a continuation of what city leaders have always done in the Black community. Even the purpose of school was significantly different for the parents and community members than for school administrators. The parents and community members made references to the school being "attractive to economic development" and a "safe place" for kids. The administrators, contrarily, did not seem to even recognize this historical framing that community members used to understand schools. And they did not seem to have any interest in understanding this, aside from describing parents as being illogical and problematic.

ADMINISTRATIVE PRIVILEGE IN SCHOOL: NEUTRAL AND POST-RACIAL

How is this case study related to culturally responsive school leadership? To understand why minoritized students are, for example, more likely to be suspended from school, or less likely to be referred to advanced placement courses, we must also understand how school educators are likely to view minoritized communities. I argue that it is unimportant whether or not educators see the community-based perspectives as "truth." Indeed, community members certainly have legitimate cause to doubt the narratives of educators. But if educators, for example, punish the way that Latinx boys talk, walk, dress, play, posture, interact, or even challenge and resist authority, we must zoom out and ask: How are educators likely to see this group of students in general? It is ahistorical, post-racial, and thus ineffective for administrators to focus on isolated data points about Black male students without understanding broader narratives and histories. It is important for district and school leaders to remember that they wield considerable "administrative privilege"; if not mindful and critically self-reflective, they will be unresponsive—and thus oppressive—toward community perspectives and needs.

This point is highlighted in Pfautz, Huguley, and McClain's historiographic study, in which they examined African American community leadership in Providence, Rhode Island. They found that Black school leaders were "socially anchored in the Black community" and that many were also "street leader[s]" whose "reputation might continue to be the most available power source."[6] Therefore, school leaders who serve urban Black communities, but who ignore the historical cultural relationships with, and behaviors of, local community leaders, may have difficulty building trust—an essential component of effective community leadership.

Historically, teachers and school leaders have always enjoyed virtually complete power and control of policy, practice, and representation around minoritized students and schools. They have had the power over what counts as knowledge, how it should be learned, who has been a successful learner, and which families have been supportive (or apathetic, or disruptive) in their children's education. Principals have also had power to define desirable and deviant behaviors in school, and to implement policies that criminalize minoritized students and communities in school. Likewise, minoritized communities also have their own interpretations, discourses, and behaviors that they exhibit toward schools. When I asked the superintendent of the district in which FDHS was located about his thoughts on the accusations of racism by Black parents, he responded: "I don't care about that. Look how the kids are performing. So, ya'll go and do your political thing. Y'all fight the political battle. I'm gonna do what's best for kids. And so, that's why I don't want to really go over there and communicate that I am making certain decisions based on race."

At just the time when a culturally responsive leadership approach could have responded to a deep, racialized, community conflict, the school leaders instead enacted a post-racial, neutral discourse. The racialized realities of the community members were neither recognized nor engaged. Recognizing the historical, oppressive structural barriers that minoritized communities face is a necessary first step to realizing culturally responsive leadership. Community-based perceptions are distinct from school-based perspectives; it is important to trace the origins of these differences, and to discuss their impact on current schooling contexts.

Safety in Administrative Behaviors: Finding Comfort in Neutrality

Unfortunately, whenever there is a threat of the unknown or a low understanding of a cultural occurrence, school leaders tend to hide behind technical-rational "administrative" behavior.[7] For example, when directly told about the community members' accusations of racism, the school principal constantly deflected the questions, saying that he could not "speak on that," or that his only job "was to improve scores and increase enrollment," or to simply "graduate kids." Should school leaders be oblivious to or uninterested in community concerns?

The administrators' posture of neutrality—such as focusing *only* on quantifiable factors and ignoring social contextual factors—was one of safety, comfort, familiarity, and control. This allowed them to safely avoid and deny the racialized claims held against them by focusing on indisputable factors, and to maintain full control of the

discourse around the school. FDHS administrators took the bureau-
cratic step of appointing a committee that would decide how the
FDHS could remain open in light of budget deficits in the district.
As the district superintendent explained,

> The membership of the, we call it the Facilities Advisory Com-
> mittee, is made up of community members. Each board member
> chose five members to represent their district and then I believe
> that gave administration . . . they gave us about five or six seats to
> fill. So, you know, the representation, the intention was to have
> equal representation from all over the district. And actually to
> be honest with you, my, my appointees were critics. You know, I
> reached out to them and to see if I could be a part of the solution
> because you're obviously very involved so you know that's, that's
> what, that's how it was made up.

Certainly, this administrator was oblivious to the claims and
sensibilities of FDHS community members. Even if the decision
to close the school was not a racial one, the administrators should
have dealt with an issue of concern within the community. But because of their intransigence and avoidance of race, and their refusal
to address the community concerns, Black residents more quickly
advanced their claims of racism. This is the *opposite* of CRSL. Given
that both the FDHS school principal and the district superintendent
were themselves people of color and yet were marginalizing the epistemologies and perspectives of a community of color, it is important
to note that all—even Black, Latinx, and Indigenous Native American—administrators need CRSL training and development!

Recognizing Administrative Power in Education and Schools

Parents and educational administrators do not have equal power
over how children are treated in school. In fact, schools tend to op-
erate almost exclusively based on how teachers and administrators

view student behaviors in school. While many educators express frustration about not being able to "get through to" or adequately serve minoritized students, many parents and students feel that they are not able to "get through to" schools. Educators have power to assign grades, discipline, and make the most critical decisions in school. They also initiate and most significantly influence how children, families, and communities are perceived. Yet parental perceptions and epistemologies are valid, and should be prioritized over schoolcentric values.

In this book, I argue that school leaders can play a pivotal role in shifting power between educators and community (i.e., students, families, community members) in equitable ways. They can choose not only to hear community voice, but also to *listen* to it, to embrace, validate, and promote it. In fact, they can lead with community voice at the center of their administrative behaviors. This is their opportunity to shift this historically school-based power to communities. Doing so should not alarm teachers. This will empower teachers to more adequately and fairly serve children from minoritized communities.

Earlier in this chapter, I recalled a comment from Betsy, a Black parent advocate who noted several historical trends that marginalized her community. In her claim that "you're going to try to take our school," she was calling out district and school leaders for ignoring community voice and making decisions devoid of community perspectives. This disproportionate power of school leaders is historically situated and one they have enjoyed from the time of colonial schooling. However, precolonial and Indigenous models of schooling did not concentrate power in the hands of school administrators.[8] Rather, these models were community based and community led, and leaders were members of that community. The activities in figure 1.1 can help us realize why power must be shared in schools.

FIGURE 1.1 Activity: Shifting and sharing power in school

It is important that identifying (or recognizing) those who have power, as well as sharing power, are institutionalized in school. This mini research project can help identify where educators wield power, how they might reduce their own power, and how students and parents can gain more power in educational settings.

Teachers' Task

1. *Sharing power.* The principal should identify a group of teachers and have them conduct mini research projects. Then, a member of the group (or principals) should ask twenty parents five basic questions such as those below. Make sure that at least half the parents are people with whom you have had very limited or no contact. Questions:

   - What am I doing well with your child?
   - What am I doing poorly or could improve on with your child?
   - Do you have a suggestion for me that would help me better educate your child?
   - What should I include in the curriculum?
     How could I treat your child more fairly?

2. *Aligning and reporting.* Were there common responses across interviews?

   - Design a plan for building this community-based data into a PLC, or professional learning community.
   - Design a plan for building this community-based data into a school improvement plan.
   - Align the data to the school district's mission and core values; suggest modifications to the mission based on the data.
   - Report out trends: Present all responses in an anonymous table.
   - Come up with a recommendation for the principal about what should change.

Principal's Task

1. Look at all of the teacher responses and find trends. Report out to all staff and make recommendations to appropriate committees about school policy changes.

2. Work with teachers to identify actionable tasks on a timeline. Some tasks might take a few months to a year, while others may require several years to complete. Still others will be ongoing and will never be "accomplished."

Superintendent's Task

1. Read the reports of all of the principals across the district; make district-level changes based on those reports.

2. Publish changes on the school's website, produce in publication format, and find other culturally responsive ways to get the message to community stakeholders.

PROBLEMS WITH "TRADITIONAL" (COLONIZING) SCHOOL LEADERSHIP MODELS

The administrators in this San Antonio area district were faced with uncertainty and discomfort from their communities, and they resorted to "policy" and raw descriptive data to make their case for closing FDHS. They were not culturally responsive in their approach, and failed to consider that schools in the United States began as places that educated the children of White elites while they cleansed and civilized minoritized people, who were seen as subhuman or deficient.[9] School leadership models were situated in colonial schooling, which meant that schools were meant to build good citizens who would contribute to the economic viability of the society. This was particularly problematic for Native American, Black, and Latinx communities because while the government prospered, these minoritized communities (and their resources) fell further behind; Whites became wealthy while Blacks and Native Americans were used to help build the nation's (White) wealth. Schools were crucial in this exploitation, and school leaders often led this charge.

What does this mean for schooling today? Because of this legacy, school leaders have difficulty breaking out of a colonizing mold. Many do not know that schools were used as weapons to cleanse Indigenous peoples of their language, customs, and spiritual beliefs and practices. A community's history is still very present for community members, and yet school leaders continue to "administer" in ways that resemble the oppressive ways of colonial administrators. The complete disregard for community voice, the lack of community epistemology in policy decisions (such as suspension policies, achievement measures, and school-community boundaries), and the sole power to make decisions about what, where, and when curricula are taught are all examples of schooling based on earlier oppressive models. In the modern era, leaders and educators are accustomed to telling minoritized communities and students how to engage with schools, and if they do not conform, they are perceived to be problematic.

Finally, there is little evidence that "traditional" leadership contributes to any significant changes to school and community. As for community, I describe in chapter 6 how most principals neither understand nor work to improve the goals and well-being of families. In other words, school resources are rarely leveraged to improve the conditions of surrounding communities. As for schooling, most principals perpetuate the policies they inherited, including oppressive practices. So when schools have oppressive practices before school leaders arrive, and those leaders do nothing to contest those practices, they will automatically be reproduced. That is why histories and the changing nature of oppression are so relevant. School leaders can lead anti-oppressive education only if they recognize the oppression in its current iteration. For example, Joshua Bornstein found that approaches like Positive Behavioral Interventions and Supports (PBIS) served to restore order, not justice, as perceptions and treatment of children of color went from their being "bad" to being "sick."[10] This means that school leaders must unearth and deeply understand their local impulses and contexts of oppression if they are to effectively contest the oppression and embrace community-based epistemologies. Otherwise, even with new "equity reforms," they will always somehow reinstate the same old oppressive practices.

Understanding the "Leadership" in CRSL

Researchers have firmly established that school leadership is one of the most important levers for positive change and reform. In recent research, my coauthors and I argue that culturally responsive school leadership is expressed in four core ways: critical self-reflection, curriculum and instruction, school context and climate, and community engagement.[11]

School-level leadership is the primary unit of analysis in this book. I focus on leaders within school buildings for a number of reasons. First, school-level leaders are best positioned to ensure that aspects of schooling can become culturally responsive. While much of the literature focuses on culturally responsive teaching and pedagogy, leadership scholars have demonstrated that whole-school reform is necessary for cultural responsiveness to be sustained. Leaders can identify sources of inequity and marginalization, and then mobilize resources to address them—of course within classrooms, but in extra-classroom and community spaces as well.

It is too hard for classroom teachers to address these goals without leadership support; leaders must provide the appropriate modeling and molding for educators to engage in this work. Several studies have demonstrated that school leadership plays a role in supporting community-based goals, improving the neighborhood community, and thus improving the lives of students.[12] In other words, leadership plays a central role in the development of the entire child, which is crucial to his or her continued academic success. Essentially, a better community member will be a better student; likewise, better students will contribute to improving the condition of their communities. In fact, a number of my prior works demonstrate that the principal is the foremost person who can galvanize a critical mass of educators in a school to confront systems of oppression that have afflicted minoritized students and communities.[13] I do not discount or ignore the power and influence that students, parents, and educators have on education within schools. But given that principals yield more power than these groups, they must recognize and use this power for the greater community good. In this way, culturally responsive school leaders are also "community leaders" as they strongly advocate for community-based goals. This advocacy empowers students—academically and socially—by strengthening opportunities for families and communities. This is in stark contrast to the isolating and constricting ways that school leadership has typically been enacted.

CONCLUSION

In this chapter, I used the case study of a proposed school closure near San Antonio, Texas, to highlight the deep fissures between community-based and schoolcentric epistemologies. While the school closure was ultimately averted by the community, district administrators and community members had different interpretations as to *why* the school was considered for closure. The community-based epistemologies were grounded in theories of racialized experiences of schooling and community life. While this chapter described behaviors of traditional school leaders who lack culturally responsive leadership, forthcoming chapters argue for positive and affirmative behaviors of culturally responsive leaders.

In San Antonio, one of the community organizers in this study, Alphonzo, a Black male student who had graduated from FDHS prior to the study, mentioned that an assistant principal at the school once held a conference with his parent. The assistant principal had mentioned that Alphonzo was a decent kid, but that he sometimes got mixed up with the wrong crowd. He mentioned that Alphonzo was a bit loud in some of his classes. His mother became defensive about her son's behaviors and wondered what school officials were going to do to help her son graduate from high school. The assistant principal didn't think that was going to be a problem, and shifted back to Alphonzo's behaviors. Alphonzo recounted to me that the meeting got intense, and that his mother and the assistant principal both left the meeting frustrated with each other.

Alphonzo and the principal had fundamentally opposing views of what was important about education. Table 1.2 helps us understand how these differences play out in school. In this table, I compare

TABLE 1.2 Competing epistemologies

Comparative issues	Community-based epistemology	Schoolcentric leadership perspective
On being "loud" in class	• "He's not loud; that's how we all speak at home." • "The students tell us all of the students are loud, but that only Black students are disciplined." • "Is he doing his work?"	• "My teachers cannot teach if he's interrupting class." • "If he's talking, he's not listening, and thus not learning." • "I gave warnings, and I will have to send him home for a few days."
On being in the "wrong" crowd	• "Who? His cousin, Todd? He needs to be around those people because they are necessary for his authentic identity? I thought this was about grades, anyway?"	• "We will define him based on who he is around." • "It's only a matter of time before he gets mixed up into something. I'll be watching out for that."
On academic achievement	• "Well, for me, I only want to know if he's going to graduate and do something positive with his life after high school."	• "Our school is evaluated based on how he, and other students, perform on the State standardized achievement test."
On parents being "defensive"; e.g.,during "tense" parent-administrator exchange	• "I know how racist this school can be because I went to it as a child." • "If you unfairly target my child, I am going to challenge, and if necessary, confront the school." • "We've got good reason to be defensive because you usually call with bad news and our kids are being picked on."	• "Some minority communities are more hostile and more tense than others." • "If parents came to the school more, their children would be doing better." • "I treat all kids equally." • "I am always very professional with parents, but they still get angry without cause."
On holding "conferences"	• "I don't always like going to the school because of how me and my siblings were treated when we were students there." (i.e., sites of trauma) • "I already know what they are gonna say, and I don't want to hear that because my son is a good kid." • "It's not easy for me to make it in because of transportation and work commitments."	• "Some parents rarely come in to see how their kids are doing in school." • "Some parents have cultural reasons they don't come in: they believe educators know best, and they leave them alone to do their jobs." • "Parents should come into schools for conferences because that's where education occurs; some communities are not safe for our teachers." • "Conferences are only about student academic progress and behavior."

how individuals of community-based and schoolcentric epistemologies approach and understand a range of issues, from students being "loud" in class to the common school practice of holding parent-teacher conferences.

Communities are neither monolithic nor static, and the community-based epistemologies in this chapter are merely one representation of a Black community in Texas. But there are multiple expressions of community-based epistemologies, which are connected to indigeneity, gender, class, race, language, religion, and ethnicity, among other markers. Even within the Black community, there are multiple markers. And for the community I studied, I only present here aspects of their protest-oriented resistance to traditional leadership models that community members saw as racist and colonizing. However, community epistemological expressions contain transcendent, decolonized, and indigenous qualities that are not strictly protest or in response to oppression. Culturally responsive school leaders must learn how to recognize these community-based expressions as well, and center these in leadership activities. In summary, there are several points of consideration for school leaders as they move away from schoolcentric perspectives and into culturally responsive leadership:

- Denial of community-based epistemologies is itself an act of oppression and will continue to contribute to inequities in school.
- Traditional forms of leadership, including schoolcentric behaviors, are linked to settler colonial forms of administration, and can be traumatic and oppressive for communities of color.
- Both community-based and schoolcentric epistemologies are unique and have historical origins, but only schoolcentric epistemologies are allowed to become policy in school. This is counter to CRSL.

- Given the historical preference for schoolcentric perspectives in school policy, priority should now be given to community-based epistemologies.
- Community-based epistemologies are not intuitive, and merely hiring principals of color will not solve the problem of marginalized community voice; on the contrary, school administrators of color can reproduce practices of oppression as well.
- Culturally responsive schools should have systematic ways of learning and discovery around the local cultural behaviors and epistemologies.

CHAPTER 1

Discussion Questions

For Principals

1. What are the current ways that community-based knowledge and epistemologies impact your practice? List three questions that you think would be helpful to talk about with your staff (i.e., questions about which you and/or your school staff would like to get smarter).

Examples of questions:
- What are adult-child boundaries in school classrooms versus in family homes?
- How might your coaches' understanding of sports participation differ from that of students and parents?
- For students who have been disciplined in school or harassed/arrested by police, how might their approach to classroom activities differ from that of White students who have not faced this type of policing?

2. How might a culturally responsive school principal have acted differently in the proposed school closure case presented in this chapter?

Questions about the case study:
- If you were to be hired at FDHS, what are three steps you would immediately take to build trust? Why (i.e., how would these steps build trust)?
- Identify a community-based cause or issue that is important to your own students/families that you could support. Explain how and why it would be important to do so.

For Teacher Leaders

1. What are strategies you can use to guide teacher colleagues who are resistant to listening to community voice?
   - Who are your critical friends and allies from whom you can seek counsel when the work becomes challenging?
   - What is your plan to continue moving forward when that happens?

2. What are ways you can meet the high-stakes accountability demands of the state and federal governments, and at the same time honor and respond to the various parents' and students' hopes and aspirations for their own communities (and schools)?

For Superintendents and District Office Staff

1. How has the district favored some community voices over others? How can the district center the most vulnerable community voices and those that are not heard at all?
2. How can you honor community voice in a way that informs policy reforms?
3. What resources can you leverage to help your school leaders recognize community voice?

"IF I HAVE TO HAVE A POLICE IN MY SCHOOL, I DON'T NEED TO BE HERE"

The Need for Critical Self-Reflective School Leaders

Always remember that the people are not fighting for ideas, nor for what is in men's minds. The people fight and accept the sacrifices demanded by the struggle in order to gain material advantages, to live better and in peace, to benefit from progress, and for the better future of their children. National liberation, the struggle against colonialism, the construction of peace, progress and independence are hollow words devoid of any significance unless they can be translated into a real improvement of living conditions.

—AMILCAR CABRAL[1]

This quote by statesman and anticolonial activist and theorist Amilcar Cabral helps us to remember that the true CRSL work is material, and not merely theoretical. CRSL reform should lead to actual material change for communities served. *Critical self-reflection* is an integral part of CRSL. In this expression of CRSL, school leaders and educators consistently look for how they are positioned within organizations that have marginalized students; they then find ways to personally and organizationally resist this oppression. The data presented in this chapter suggests that this oppression can be explicit—such as outright exclusionary practices affecting minoritized students, or implicit—such as teachers accepting "misbehaving" students from other classes into their classrooms, which supports their colleagues' exclusionary behaviors toward students. Several useful tools promoted in past research have pushed school leaders to be more critically self-reflective; scholars have written about completing "racial autobiographies" and having conversations around the types of privilege that principals enjoy, for example. Certainly some of these are valuable tools. But in this chapter I suggest that personal critical self-reflection is not enough. I argue that all structures and processes in schools need to be critically self-reflective as well. So in the same way that we (educators) must ask how we are personally responsible for reproducing oppressive practices, we must also critically examine the role of our school programs, departments, hiring practices, enrichment courses, and other school structures.

Because schools automatically reproduce oppressive structures unless challenged, it is important for us to look at how culturally responsive leaders initiate processes of critical self-reflection for the entire school and district. In an earlier literature review, my colleagues and I offered the following about the important role of critical self-reflection:[2]

> We found a number of works referred to the notion that the leader needed to have *an awareness of self and his/her values, beliefs, and/or dispositions when it came to serving poor children of color*. This is also referred to as a critical consciousness, and we suggest that this awareness can be developed. A good leadership preparation program that addresses race, culture, language, national identity, and other areas of difference is necessary but not sufficient in developing a critical consciousness.

The data in this chapter suggests that school leaders who practice CRSL constantly seek, find, *and challenge* oppressive treatment of students and communities, and they push their staff to do so as well. Remember, CRSL is a process that cannot be completed. Rather, it is a dynamic, fluid set of behaviors that regularly (re)develop the individual and the organization based on a steady stream of data from the school and community. To be sure, some teachers will challenge

CRSL and types of critical self-reflection. In this chapter, I look at how Joe critically reflected upon multiple aspects of schooling, and how these aspects impacted UAHS students. I describe the responses of teachers—both resistant and supportive—and how the principal institutionalized CRSL and incorporated teacher sensibilities in the work. Joe seemed to have a working knowledge of how oppression existed and minoritized students—in both the school and the district, as well as in the society at large—and frequently put that in front of his staff and students. At the outset, it is important to note that I believe leaders must consider the following three skills as they regularly renew their commitment to be critically self-reflective:

1. The ability to identify and understand the oppressive contexts that students and their communities face;
2. The willingness and humility to identify and vocalize one's own personal background and privilege, which allows leaders to see how they are directly involved or complicit in oppressive contexts; and
3. The courage to push colleagues and staff to critically self-reflect upon their personal and professional role in oppression and anti-oppressive works, and to eventually develop responsive school structures.

For culturally responsive school leaders, these three necessary skills should eventually lead to concrete actions to develop culturally responsive schools through critical self-reflection.

WHAT DATA SHOULD BE USED TO CRITICALLY SELF-REFLECT?

It is important to use both school data (student, teacher, program, and schoolwide data) and community data (parent, community, and student voice) in self-reflecting. When I began my research in Davistown,

Michigan, minoritized students were being severely underserved. The traditional school measures and data of student outcomes looked stark—the graduation rate, standardized testing data, grade retention, class and grade failure rate, suspension rate, referrals to special education, referrals to gifted and talented classes, and the extended number of years that students held ELL status, among other data, all looked bleak for minoritized students. For example, in recent data for the district, Black students made up only 18 percent of students overall, but nearly 60 percent of out-of-school suspensions. And on state standardized exams, they typically scored between 20 and 30 percent less on state-mandated achievement tests. As covered in chapter 1, this type of equity data is not unique to Davistown. Similarly, like other cities and districts, educators and other stakeholders in Davistown seemed concerned about such data.

Perhaps more troubling, however, was other, equally crucial data—the narratives that students and parents shared about their schools and teachers. It became clear from community narratives of Indigenous, Black, Brown, ELL, and other minoritized students that they were not being served.

Why Is Critical Self-Reflection Dynamic?

Racism and other types of oppression are so ubiquitous that they are often rendered invisible, or considered normal. But they are also ever-morphing, and privilege is self-protective and reentrenching. Critical self-reflection allows leaders to see how oppression and marginalization is happening, *now*—and to catch it as it newly positions itself in organizations.

The lack of critical self-reflection, unfortunately, leads to a muting of community voice. This muting, or even erasure, provides an opportunity for school leaders to deny their role in oppression of some communities, and to blame the students and communities for poor school performance and disciplinary problems. It is up to school leaders to decide whether or not they will be anti-oppressive in their behaviors. I pull from the works of Gooden and Dantley and Capper, Theoharis, and Sebastian, as well as my own works; this collective research makes it clear that administrators will either resist or reproduce and reify oppression that is already present in schools.[3] School leaders who choose to remain neutral about marginalized student populations cannot become culturally responsive. This chapter recounts how Joe, the UAHS school principal, was reflective about ways that he and his staff were serving (or underserving) children. Research suggests impactful critical self-reflection is an iterative process that involves personal and structural reflections in a constant state of change, combating the ever-morphing systems of oppression that our students face.[4] The questions in figure 2.1 illustrate how this

FIGURE 2.1 How do I lead critical self-reflection? Locating and resisting oppression

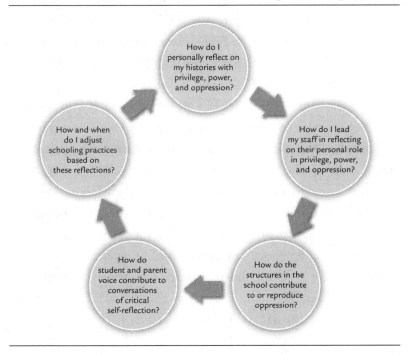

process looked at UAHS, and the forthcoming sections discuss the shift from personal to institutional self-reflection.

PERSONAL REFLECTION OF SCHOOL LEADERS

Joe regularly reflected on his own history and his current practices as a way to measure his personal involvement in the oppression of schools. These reflections were both public and private, and he was cognizant of the fact that he was over seventy, while most of his students were under eighteen. In one interview early in the study, he pushed me (as the researcher) to "interview the kids and their parents, and ask them directly. And tell me what they said, because I ain't perfect, and I can change." This was a rare type of humility in which a principal was regularly asking students and parents what he could do better to properly serve their children.

In one extended conversation Joe had in his office, a parent was critical of Joe's use of profanity with her student. Keisha was the parent of a newer ninth-grade student and had problems with some of Joe's interactions with students: "I am not trying to say anything negative, but I'm gonna be honest with you since you asked: I teach my kids to respect all people, and not to use foul language. And when it's used so freely here by you, it is disrespectful." For her, it was about making sure that her Black student felt valued and respected, and she had brought her child to this school because that was what she expected from UAHS. Joe not only acknowledged this concern, but also acknowledged the *validity* of the voice: "I hear ya, and I agree. I did want to let you know that we meet students where they are, instead of where we think they *should* be. The students use this type of language, and they are more in their element with those who know how to use their language. But I hear what you're saying." While Joe's response could be contested and critiqued, one thing was clear: he was willing to engage and reflect in critical conversations with parents about the treatment of minoritized children.

CENTERING MINORITIZED STUDENT VOICE

Joe not only made space for student voice in school, but he also used that student voice to challenge marginalizing opinions and oppressive practices of UAHS teachers. At UAHS, "centering" student voice involved educators' using student experiences and epistemologies as a source of valuable knowledge that impacts content, policy, and practice. During one of my first visits to UAHS, Joe introduced me to a junior named Marwan. Marwan was a 1.5-generation (i.e., his family immigrated to the US when he was a child) Palestinian American student who had been pressured to leave his assigned high school because teachers considered him to be "too hyper." But it became clear to me that he was brilliant. Marwan was involved in local rap groups, and though his mother did not speak English well, he was one of the most lyrically talented local hip-hop performers that I had ever witnessed. He offered freestyle raps—impromptu raps that are constructed on the spot in rhythmic fashion, have new content, and are often about an unplanned topic—and constructed beats (instrumental songs) in ways that most could appreciate. He and several other talented rappers, mostly other UAHS students, would perform at local street festivals and venues. Here is an exchange in which Joe was meeting with Marwan and one of the UAHS science teachers, Rhonda. Rhonda had first told Marwan to wait outside of her class, then to go to another teacher's classroom for the remainder of the hour. She was a middle-aged White woman who didn't seem to be aware of any of Marwan's talents, nor did she seem interested in them. Rhonda simply said he was disruptive toward other students, and she later requested a meeting with the principal (Joe). I attended the meeting, and recorded the following exchange:

MARWAN: I don't like going to Rhonda's class because she be yellin' at me for no reason, and then she tries to put me out.

JOE: Yeah, but what are *you* doing in class for her to do that?

MARWAN: Nothin', I swear!

RHONDA: Yup, that's about right, nothin! You sit and don't complete your work and then you disturb other students in class!

JOE: Wait, let him finish! Now if what Rhonda says is true, why *do* you deserve to be here?

MARWAN: Well, first of all, it's not true. If it's true, how I gotta B in her class? And secondly, I ain't finta let nobody disrespect me.

This dialogue continued for a while. When Joe asked Marwan why he felt he deserved to *not* be excluded from Rhonda's class, or from school, Marwan explained: "Well, I'm still doing my work, plus everybody be talkin' in there. But she forget about all of them, and she just go in on [i.e., targets] me for no reason." It may seem obvious to us why students should be in school and in class, but Joe felt it necessary to guide the student voice to respond directly to the teacher's exclusionary behaviors. In other words, Joe asked a question of the student that directly challenged the exclusionary impulses of the teacher. After Joe heard each perspective and had allowed Rhonda and Marwan to respond in an equitable manner, he eventually weighed in: "He needs to be in that classroom so that he can learn."

After the three met together, Joe met with each person individually. In his private meeting with Joe, Marwan insisted that he was wronged; Joe acknowledged Marwan's feelings and perceptions: "We will take care of that" (i.e., Rhonda's picking on him). But Joe also took the opportunity to push Marwan toward being more focused in class, and more respectful toward his teachers. So while Joe acknowledged Marwan's voice of protest about exclusionary behaviors directed toward him by his teacher, he also challenged Marwan to embrace and reflect on his own classroom behaviors. This practice of giving space for students to speak directly about ways they feel oppressed is crucial to CRSL.

In the meeting with Rhonda, Joe explained that while she might have some legitimate concerns about Marwan's behaviors, "removal from classrooms helps no one; you've got to work with the students and you can't do that when they're not here." While promising Rhonda that he would personally work with Marwan, he used Marwan's voice to resist Rhonda's behaviors, which, according to Joe, "were the same types of pushout behaviors that Marwan had been experiencing for years." Joe explained that the teachers and principal in Marwan's previous traditional school had a relationship that seemed to confirm schoolcentric perspectives and to devalue or dismiss student viewpoints. In contrast, Joe used the student's voice and perspective to push Rhonda to reflect on how she may have been a part of exclusionary (oppressive) practices toward a student in her class.

USING "CENTERED" STUDENT VOICE TO INFORM CRITICAL SELF-REFLECTION

Direct Principal-Student Relationships

Unlike educators in most schools, UAHS teachers were placed into direct conversation with students about how they were oppressive toward their students. This occurred in a manner that did not place the onus of anti-oppressive work on students (or parents), but rather in a way that allowed student and parent voices to impact how policy and practice happened at UAHS. Students enjoyed the opportunity and spoke freely about how they felt they were treated. They believed that this gave them courage and self-confidence. But above all, they were experiencing something they felt they never had in school: fairness and a sense of belonging. But how did conversations around student marginalization and oppression take place at UAHS?

The first way that these conversations occurred was by allowing UAHS students direct and uninhibited access to the principal. This access meant not only physical proximity, but also the ability to express their positions on educational or personal matters. Whether at the beginning or end of the school day, during lunch, or during hallway passing time, any student in the school could stop Joe and indicate that they needed to speak with him in private. Parents stopped him as well. There were no limits to what they could discuss, and roughly half of the forty-three meetings I observed were directly related to how students felt they were being treated in school. The second way that anti-oppressive conversations took place at UAHS was through town-hall-style meetings held every Wednesday, called rap sessions.

Critique in Public Space: Use of Rap Sessions

In addition to his direct relationships with students and families, Joe implemented a unique way of institutionalizing self-reflection. Rap sessions were schoolwide, all-inclusive meetings whereby students, teachers, parents, the principal, and all other staff engaged in critical conversations about behaviors in the school—and not just student behaviors. These rap sessions took place in the middle of the octagon-shaped school. Though parents almost always attended and spoke their truths about the teachers, school, district, or even Joe, the rap sessions mainly served as a space to let students speak directly about their teachers and learning experiences. Here is how Joe characterized them, just after a rap session in which a student sternly critiqued how a teacher had treated him:

> It lets kids express themselves and reminds them of their responsibilities . . . It relieves some of their frustration. It gets them together as a group to talk about commonalities. You talk about dos and don'ts. You talk about loving each other, you talk about respecting each other. You can talk about anything you want to talk about. Talk about boys taking advantage of girls, sex. But in the end, most of them [students] take responsibility for their own actions and for what happens here at the school.

Rap sessions were a consistent venue for Joe to allow students to explain their perceptions of their treatment. For example, in one instance, Tony, a Black student previously on criminal probation, forcefully exclaimed that his teacher "be acting like she be pickin' on me and that she don't care if I make it or not." Joe cut in firmly, "And even if she is, you've gotta first believe in yourself. And sometimes Tony, it doesn't seem like you do that." Finally, Joe let Tony know that "we will take care of that."

In many cases, Joe provided advice and encouragement to individual students to change delinquent behaviors, as seen here. But he always listened to the students and responded to their issues, as shown in his response of "we will take care of that." The mutually occupied spaces for students, staff, and parents that the principal created simultaneously challenged students to embrace and reflect on their own behaviors, while giving them a voice to discuss the exclusionary behaviors directed toward them by teachers.

Improving Practices and Policy with Student Voice

While rap sessions are only one example of an administrative practice intended to engage community-based epistemologies and perceptions, the *intent* of rap sessions must exist in all schools. That is, schools must find ways to present community-based perspectives as real and valuable, and thus, as a way to induce critical self-reflection in staff (and to critique their own epistemologies and perspectives). This activity does not need to be a rap session, but it must be a practice that places community-based perspectives and knowledge at the center of school reform. At UAHS, the rap sessions allowed students to have a direct influence on their own educational inclusion and policy. In one instance, Joe used a student comment about noise level to push his colleagues in a staff meeting: "Well, like Michael said in rap session, talking loud is not a reason for a student to be sent to the office, because that's how some of them talk at home." The meetings inserted the student voice into Joe's policy decisions; that is, student and parent narratives from the rap sessions would impact how staff meetings happened. In countless staff meetings, student voices were used as data to push staff toward deeper self-reflection.

Rap sessions also pushed students to critically self-reflect on their current behaviors and future plans. Moreover, they allowed Joe to encourage certain student behaviors that he and his staff thought were important, and he would have very public conversations about how students, too, should be critically self-reflective about their own future. The following excerpt comes from field notes I took of a rap session dialogue between Joe and UAHS senior, Howard:

> Howard was a graduating senior who was before the group, and started by proclaiming, "Yes! I'm finally 'bout to be done!" Joe responded, "Yeah, but tell 'em what you doing now [i.e., after graduation]." So, in front of the whole school, Joe was encouraging the student to share his accomplishments and future plans. Howard quickly added, "I'll be startin' at Southern College [pseudonym] in the fall." One of Howard's friends jeered, "Man, you ain't goin' nowhere!" and a group of students in the rap session audience broke into laughter. Joe jumped in: "Shut up, we're

bein' serious here!" The responses of the students allowed for critical self-reflection on both positive and negative academic and social behaviors.

This dialogue between Howard, Joe, and the entire UAHS community allowed Howard to conceptualize his future plans; a far cry from exclusionary education, it also served as practice for students who were beginning to positively affirm their academic identities, and to articulate to educators their educational plans. Joe's encouragement of Howard to "tell 'em what you doing now" was a way to develop self-advocacy among his students. This administrative behavior (i.e., the rap session), along with the constant encouragement for students to share their perspectives and accomplishments, imbued the school culture with a sense of inclusiveness. Through peer observation and mimicking, students learned how to advocate for themselves, and used the opportunity to also advocate for or resist issues they were facing. Those same student and parent voices would almost always enter discussions that staff had about disciplinary, programmatic, and even academic policies. The result was that students felt a sense of belonging and empowerment in school. Howard and his classmates said that, for the first time ever, adults in buildings "listened to what we said and made changes." Consequently, one of Howard's most frequent comments was that he "trusted Joe." He and his classmates, who resisted and suspiciously viewed other educators (with good reason), were willing to learn from teachers at UAHS and take guidance from its principal.

Using Community-Based Epistemology in Critical Self-Reflection

The spaces that Joe opened up in the school allowed raw and unfiltered community voices into school activities and policy making. This access to the sharing of perspectives and personal stories, as well as complaints and compliments about UAHS, the staff, the district, or the community all contributed to how the staff viewed the school and the contexts in which students lived. For example, in one meeting, a grandparent and guardian of a UAHS senior sternly critiqued the treatment of African American children in the district. She said that the teachers in the district did not know how to "teach" and "love on" Black kids. She said that all Black parents she knew were "constantly having run-ins with the school" because of the teachers' treatment of Black kids. While the grandparent's comments were not directed at UAHS and did not lead to any particular policy discussions, such public comments contributed to how UAHS staff taught and perceived students. They also contributed to staff understanding of how they could either resist or be complicit in structural oppressions that UAHS students faced.

This freedom to share unfiltered and unpoliced perspectives was an experience that students and parents had never had in their traditional schools and classrooms. But these "safe" conversations allowed for a deep engagement of community epistemologies. Uncontrolled, authentic conversations allowed tensions to emerge. And they caused teachers to think more deeply about whether they were actually further marginalizing the UAHS children. Critical self-reflection therefore became a part of the institutional structure at UAHS (see figure 2.2).

FROM PERSONAL TO STRUCTURAL: INSTITUTIONALIZING CRITICAL SELF-REFLECTION

Much of the literature on critical self-reflection and self-awareness emphasizes personal identities and teacher positionalities. In other works, my colleagues and I argue that critical self-reflection is one of four areas of culturally responsive school leadership.[5] Critical conversations around race, personal roles that educators have had in oppressive schooling, and racial autobiographies have been some of the

FIGURE 2.2 Activity (60–90 days): Institutionalizing antibias practice

1. Principal should form antibias work groups with teachers and instructional support staff (provide incentives for volunteers). Invest in mini cameras with digital video recording (DVR) capabilities. Record instructional classroom time. Randomly select videos of teachers during class periods, and view and discuss the videos in a large group. Look for patterns of teacher behavior in response to students. Discussion questions: Which students are most often in contact with the teacher? What are the characteristics of those students? Which students are most often called on to answer questions? Which students are most likely to be disengaged in the classroom? Whose culture is most represented in the classroom curriculum, instruction, and teaching? Which students are most likely to be disciplined? Sent out of the classroom? Referred to special education?

2. Next identify and report out trends. Use supporting material such as referrals to further establish the trends.

3. Last, come up with a recommendation for the principal about what should change.

Principal's Task

All building administrators work together as one team. Look for bias trends in administrative behavior. Write a daily journal that describes your interactions with students and parents, and every month, share it with a team member. Look for differences in how you respond to some student groups. If a discipline gap exists in the school, that is an administrative responsibility. Do trends of bias exist in principal interactions? Establish evidence for how you answer the question.

Superintendent's Task

While working with the antibias teaching group formed in step 1, view recordings of school board meetings and look for similar patterns in how various parents, administrators, or other stakeholders are treated. Are some given preference over others? Do trends of bias exist in board meetings? Establish evidence for how you answer the question.

foci of administrators and teachers engaged in critical self-reflection. This work has been valuable for teachers and schools. However, for culturally responsive schooling to become systemic and institutionalized, this work must be expanded in two crucial ways. First, critical self-reflection must be embedded into the horizontal structures of schooling; that is, the work must occur more than once per year when school and district equity data is released. Rather, it must be woven throughout all of the tools and processes that schools use, including administrative observations and walk-throughs, referrals of *any* kind (e.g., disciplinary, special education testing, advanced and gifted and talented classes, remedial classes, student and parent leadership roles), and meeting agendas, among other tools.

Second, critical self-reflection must align with vertical structures of culturally responsive schooling. In other words, school leaders must ensure that resource allocation, employment decisions, school climate, relationships with district administration and policies, and community engagement are also culturally responsive. All of these structures will either support or challenge oppressive structures that are already in schools. This research at UAHS suggests that school leaders are responsible for initiating and sustaining this work.

CONCLUSION

A first and continuing act of culturally responsive school leadership is critical self-reflection. This is a necessary first step because it is a process through which school leaders recognize and discover how their institutions and practices have been oppressive to minoritized students. This chapter showed how Joe, a culturally responsive school principal, enacted specific leadership behaviors that led staff to be more critically self-reflective and aware of their privilege and their oppressive behaviors toward minoritized students. One teacher, Rhonda, first expressed frustration during a dialogue in which Joe seemed to give equal credibility to her and Marwan's statements; but in a follow-up interview she conceded, "Joe tries to be fair, and sometimes it's like, are you going to stand up and lead this school or not? But I see why he's doing it, and I know that I may be doing things too that I've got to change because I don't understand the lives of students, and I could learn more." Joe constantly reminded his staff of the perspectives of students and parents. Whether through personal conversations or schoolwide meetings, the centering of community epistemology and voice was a useful tool that Joe used to engage UAHS staff in becoming self-reflective.

Self-Advocacy: Supporting Student Self-Reflection

Another aspect frequently left out of CRSL is how principals can foster self-reflection in students. At UAHS, Joe did this in two ways. First, he created opportunities for students to express how they have been marginalized in school. This built trust. And as we discussed, this was a crucial way that UAHS teachers came to understand their role in marginalizing students. But centering student voice was directly useful to students as well. It allowed them to reflect on their own behaviors and future plans without feeling patronized or policed. Joe's advocacy of student voice and perspectives is highlighted throughout this text, but it is particularly relevant to chapters 3 and 4. Joe also encouraged students to be critically self-reflective and consider how they might improve their own behaviors and the well-being of their communities.

Impact of Critical Self-Reflection

Principals' leading with critical self-reflection has a tremendous impact on the education of minoritized students. In my twenty years of education, I had not witnessed students and parents describe principals and teachers as "fair." The school leaders' and educators' willingness to discuss, openly, how they had been complicit in marginalizing students made them credible in the minds of students and parents. Their willingness to advocate for community-based causes (which is taken up later in this book) only added to this credibility. Students' and parents' perceptions of UAHS staff as fair made all the difference for the students' own educational experiences. They were willing to be vulnerable with the teachers; they did not feel the need to defend themselves against oppressive educators. They were willing to accept the leadership of Joe and the actions of UAHS teachers. Indeed, all teachers and principals think they are always acting in the best interests of students; but because of the histories and complicity (or even silence) of schools in the oppression of minoritized communities, many community members and students come into schools with their guard up. However, at UAHS, when students and parents witnessed regular conversations about racism, discussions of racial equity data, and advocacy for their community-based causes, trust was built. Rap sessions and other public meetings allowed community and student voices to be heard, and they then saw UAHS policies changed based on their voices. As I discussed earlier, many scholars and researchers position "trust" and "a sense of belonging" as among the primary reasons that minoritized students experience school pushout. The UAHS students remained in school, identified as good students, graduated, and mostly continued with their education.

What More Must Be Done?

While centering community-based perspectives in school practices and behaviors is important, it is not enough. This is true because parents, students, and community members may not have an in-depth working knowledge of all school processes, such as the recruitment and retention of minoritized staff or how to leverage federal funding for equity and justice in schooling. For a more comprehensive way of finding oppressive practices and structures in school, I recommend equity audits. Some models of equity audits include researched-based surveys as well as data and policy analysis functions that look specifically at how oppression continues to happen within schools (based on prior research studies) and the ways that students, parents, and communities are marginalized.[6]

This chapter highlighted how critical self-reflection of CRSL happens in various "spaces." CRSL spaces of critical reflection are locations within and around the school where issues of oppression seem to persist. Oppression is deeply connected with privilege, and scholars such as George Lipsitz have effectively argued that we must all be cognizant of our privilege and use tit to fight for the rights of the oppressed.[7]

Table 2.1 considers questions to help disentangle privilege from oppression, particularly as it happened at UAHS. The table also helps us understand how critical self-reflection can be institutionalized in various ways. It is imperative that CRSL building and district leaders find ways to promote institutions that are critically self-reflective. While this is an ongoing goal that will never fully be attained, there must be systematic ways by which leaders show that they are constantly aware of how they may be reproducing oppression, and how they can combat it.

TABLE 2.1 Moving toward institutional critical self-reflection

Types/spaces of critical self-reflection	Critical questions
Personal critical self-reflection	• How have I enjoyed privilege over other groups, especially those that I serve in my school? • How do I continue to benefit from systemic privileges that I did not earn? • How have I contributed to the oppression of groups I serve? • Do I share our racial background in school and other public places, and use it as an opportunity to discuss racial oppression?
Content critical self-reflection	• Am I aligning my discussions and agenda items at staff meetings with equity? • Do I support staff in their lesson planning and CRSL curriculum development? • Are communications with parents in their native language? Does communication reflect their epistemologies and interests? • How do I ensure that messages from the school are accountable to and representative of community-based perspectives and interests? • How do I know if my teachers are using student experiences and community epistemology throughout their classroom curriculum and learning materials?

continues

TABLE 2.1 *Continued*

Types/spaces of critical self-reflection	Critical questions
Structural critical self-reflection	• Do I leverage school resources in ways that center the needs of minoritized students? • Is my program regularly examined to identify how we are marginalizing or disadvantaging students? • Are programs—such as special education, ELL, and remedial tracks—disproportionately and negatively impacting minoritized students? • Do minoritized students have access to the same social capital networks as nonminoritized students?
Community-based critical self-reflection	• How am I including parent (or caregiver) voice in school governance and policy making? • Do parents feel comfortable in this school? • To what extent do the staff and the focus of school dialogue reflect the community being served?
Organizational critical self-reflection	• Am I hiring staff who are consistent with community demographics and who are willing to be self-reflective around issues of oppression? • Am I ensuring that I hire staff who have embraced (or will agree to embrace) anti-oppression and antiracism? • Am I criticizing and overlooking minoritized candidates for reasons that go unnoticed in White middle-class teacher candidates? • Do I get the necessary support from the district to do CRSL work?
Sustainable critical self-reflection	• In what ways do I routinely and systematically ask the questions in this chart (and others like them)? • How do I make my staff, my institution, and myself accountable to these (and similar) questions? • How am I tracking culturally responsive leadership and teaching consistently throughout the school year?

CHAPTER 2

Discussion Questions

For Principals

1. In what ways do you institutionalize critical self-reflection in your school? How can you strengthen this institutionalization across the multiple types/spaces of critical self-reflection?
2. How do community epistemologies impact the policies in your school?
3. Site Improvement Plan for Critical Self-Reflection of the Organization. Bring your plan to a group of colleagues and critique it based on the ideas in the introduction, chapter 1, and chapter 2 in this book.

For Teacher Leaders and Equity Leadership Teams

1. What is a brief activity that you can do during *every meeting* to give staff an opportunity for critical self-reflection?
2. The centering of student and community voice—and giving that voice equal weight in decision making and policy in a school—is something that makes many teachers feel uncomfortable. How would the equity team build both trust and allies with staff in your building?

For Superintendents and District Office Staff

1. How do you support your principals/buildings and central office administrators in being critically self-reflective (for example, to look deeply for ways they may be reproducing oppression or what they might need from you to enact equity audits)?
2. What will be the sanctions for administrators who lead schools that have persistent issues of oppression, and who do not provide evidence that they are actively trying to combat them?

"I CAN'T HELP THEM IF THEY'RE NOT HERE"

Promoting Inclusive Spaces for Minoritized Youth

A central premise of this book is that schools automatically reproduce systems of privilege or oppression, even without intentional effort or thought. If school leaders remain neutral—claiming that they did not personally initiate the system, or that they have policies or intentions that are not oppressive and that promote inclusion—then the oppressive structures and practices will almost certainly be reproduced in the schools they lead. Thus, school leaders will not only be complicit in continuing oppressive practices, but will be active reproducers of such practices. In this chapter, I argue that culturally responsive school leaders must protect and promote the practices that include minoritized students and the spaces in which they exist. This requires active stances and behaviors of anti-oppression. If asked, most principals would likely say that their goal is to lead an inclusive environment. But how can this happen if leaders and staff do not understand how identities and communities are minoritized, and can neither recognize these spaces nor understand how to promote their inclusion within schools? Research time and again has demonstrated that schools are often not inclusive of minoritized students, and thus they do not feel a sense of belonging in school.

WHAT IS INCLUSIVE SPACE?

Space and identity are tightly connected and in chapter 4, I demonstrate how minoritized identities are marginalized and how culturally responsive school leaders promote environments that embrace student identity and voice. However, here in chapter 3, I focus on the school space, and how school leaders must embrace inclusionary school practice. The word *space* indicates not only physical location, but also social and historical contexts that are associated with communities. In other words, bodies with unique local histories occupy particular spaces. Those collective memories remain with the bodies therein. Space is not only about student bodies, but also encompasses epistemologies, behaviors, and artifacts associated with distinct minoritized communities. So, for example, Latinx male students' patterns of language, dress, interactive behaviors, relationships with authority, value of education, and ways of learning are all associated with Latinx communities. This is true whether or not a particular Latinx male student is actually from a Latinx community, or whether such behaviors are even truly typical of Latinx males. The public imagination superimposes historical understandings on Latinx males. Susan Katz explains: "Latino students face teachers who perceive them through the stereotype of 'gang-banger,' within a system of tracking that places them as non-native speakers of English in the bottom rung."[1] In other words, since teachers in the United States already have a historical understanding of Latinx males that is tightly connected to the Latinx community, they will understand those students through their narrow, and likely stereotypical, lenses. In this chapter, I am concerned not only with what students bring from their spaces, but also with how educators see and react to spaces and associated bodies.

In this study, I address how the minoritized students were routinely pushed out of traditional schools that had designed school space to exclusively accommodate middle-class White students. As I discuss the notion of space, it is important to remember that space, and how it is connected with people, has real meaning for students in school. If students are connected with certain spaces, they are less welcome in school. Gupta and Ferguson suggest that "identity of a place emerges by the intersection of its specific involvement in a system of hierarchically organized spaces with its cultural construction as a community or locality."[2] Based on Gupta and Ferguson and other scholarly works, I suggest the following:[3]

- Children from Indigenous, Black, Brown, poor, and other minoritized students are connected to particular spaces.
- Even when they are not connected to certain spaces, educators still see them as belonging to or having emerged from these spaces.
- These spaces are contested—and have been formed by institutional structures like colonialism, land dispossession, confinement and slavery, ghettoization, mass incarceration, and federal and state policy.
- Minoritized and Indigenous peoples have been impacted by these systems of oppression, and these spaces have often been the locus for that oppression.
- Oppression is not confined to spaces, however, and thus even when students emerge from their space, they are still seen as belonging to that space, and therefore face similar types of oppression even outside of those spaces.
- Minoritized spaces are not bad, and many students take pride in their spaces.
- Minoritized spaces are seen as spaces that must be confined and controlled; they have been marginalized in US society, as have been all students who are seen as belonging to those spaces. Even so, people in these spaces have value and agency, and have

appropriated, adapted, transcended, and both claimed and resisted these spaces and associated systems of oppression.
- Most schools do not recognize the value associated with minoritized spaces, and therefore often maintain society's oppression of such space.

The UAHS principal is unique because he not only recognized
the value of minoritized spaces—in his words, "the community"—
but he also made sure that he and his staff maintained a presence in
those spaces. Likewise, he prevented the school from excluding students, artifacts, languages, other people, and even behaviors associated with any particular type of space, particularly Black, Latinx, and
other minoritized spaces. While code words like "publicly assisted
housing" and "urban areas" were used by staff, Joe rejected the exclusionary impulses that some of his teachers displayed that would most
often pressure students out of school. Instead, he mentored and encouraged teachers toward inclusiveness. And at times, he challenged
his teachers to accept behaviors that some teachers personally found
distasteful or even incompliant with school policy and expectations.
Joe's widening of the school space was a core part of his inclusionary school culture, and this inclusiveness ultimately contributed to
student comfort and school completion. This chapter discusses the
*practices that Joe and other culturally responsive school leaders use to pro-
mote school as an inclusive space*, with a focus on educator practices
and school-based processes that impact the inclusion or exclusion of
students from school.

WHAT ARE EXCLUSIONARY PRACTICES
AND WHY DO THEY HAPPEN?

Exclusionary practices of schooling are actions by principals, educators, and other staff that contribute to students not being present in

school. *Direct exclusionary practices* in schooling include the explicit removal of students from the classroom, such as

- in-school suspensions
- out-of-school suspensions
- in-school detention
- zero-tolerance and other permanent exclusion policies
- use of law enforcement policies against students
- allowing students to miss class, or school altogether, without repercussion
- student deal making (i.e., allowing students to disengage from learning)

In addition to these direct, short-term exclusionary practices, there are long-term, *less direct exclusionary practices* that are so hostile that children are eventually pressured out of school. In these cases, students are not explicitly removed from school, but are "pushed out." Researchers such as Okey and Cusick as well as Dei and colleagues find that educators and administrators exert so much pressure on some students that they choose not to stay in school.[4] Some common indirect exclusionary behaviors in school include

- grade retention
- constant disciplinary referrals
- not being welcoming to parents and community members
- not engaging minoritized neighborhoods/communities
- not valuing non-White behavior, cultural capital, aesthetic, language, or dress
- hostile treatment (e.g., ridiculing, harassment, denial of oppression, and ignoring)
- emotional abuse (e.g., shaming, teasing, tokenizing, and dismissiveness)

- constant critique in school and class of only certain types of students
- allowing student disengagement

Both direct and less-direct exclusionary practices are protean and dynamic, always shifting to resituate power into the hands of those who have always had power; in schools, those with the power to label as deviant and exclude children have always been administrators and teachers.

By offering examples of student behaviors that are often punished, table 3.1 can help educators distinguish between exclusionary and inclusionary responses.

My past research along with that of scholars like Picower and Solomon et al. suggests that those with power do not like to cede power; it must be understood that policy *alone* cannot address exclusionary practices of educators.[5] It must be accompanied by critical self-reflection and other aspects of anti-oppressive staff training. In this book, I argue that the principal and other administrators are not only best positioned, but also most responsible for ensuring that both school policy and practice are nonexclusionary (i.e., anti-oppressive) for minoritized students. Here are two common questions that I am asked while in schools working with administrators, and my responses:

1. *Questioner*: "How can we [educators] know what culturally responsive practices are best for our students, especially with regard to student misconduct?"
2. *My response*: "'Misbehaving' is socially constructed within your school. How have you included the parents and other community members in how you define *misbehavior*?"
3. *Questioner*: "What should we do with our zero-tolerance policy? Our hands are tied! Do we *have* to remove some students?"
4. *My response*: "First, if you do not like zero-tolerance policies, then use your power to advocate against them. Second, you

TABLE 3.1 Inclusive and exclusive school space

This activity will help educators link school space to inclusivity and exclusivity in current research.

Examples of student behaviors in school space	Exclusionary practices	Inclusionary practices
Student sleeping in classroom	Criticize or make fun of student; discipline student and send to the office.	Allow student to come to classroom during off-hours to complete work; work with other staff to help student get proper rest at home.
Underage student smelling like marijuana	Remove student from classroom or school.	Work with staff to ensure student has access to substance treatment programs, if needed.
Student perceived as acting "aggressive"	Discipline student with referral or in-school or out-of-school suspension.	Welcome the student behaviors and discover ways the student can use the behaviors in learning activities. If behavior modification is needed, ask the student and parents the best way to help the student improve behaviors.
Student using the n word (i.e., *nigga*)	Shame and critique the student's use of the word by saying things like: "How can you expect anyone else to stop calling you a nigger, if you use the term on yourselves?"	Understand that this is cultural speech, and you are not in a strong position to determine what is legitimate cultural speech for others. Have consistent rules across groups—including White middle-class students—about the use of cultural speech; help students understand that there are times when it may be unwise for them to use such language.
Student not following directions (i.e., insubordination)	Gossip with other teachers about how bad the student is; then gather collective support to target and suspend the student.	Recognize this leadership behavior in the student, and insist that he join leadership activities in the classroom and school.

continues

TABLE 3.1 *Continued*

Examples of student behaviors in school space	Exclusionary practices	Inclusionary practices
Student fighting	Suspend students; require parents to attend conference in school before students return.	Require the feuding students to complete a community engagement project together, and then have students cowrite a report demonstrating how such work enriches the community. School leaders should provide transportation if needed as well as childcare for younger siblings if that is a barrier to completing the project.
Student late or skipping class	Remove student from school for truancy.	Enlist the support of community elders—experienced community members who maintain and pass on knowledge and culture to help mentor the student into attending class.

should know that there are large racial and class gaps in how zero-tolerance policies (and similarly, the death penalty) are applied. If you are Black, Indigenous, Latinx, or poor, you are far more likely to have zero-tolerance policies applied against you than if you are White and middle-class. This indicates that there is great discretion in how and when districts apply the policy. I have been an educational administrator long enough to know that when districts (and schools) really want to find ways around a policy, they know just how to do so."

Finally, I use this chapter to show that the wealth of knowledge and practice from communities must be centered on inclusionary educational approaches. School leadership with community can help school leaders and staff to understand the powerful ancestral and community-based knowledge that can actually help educators to be more inclusive. In table 3.2, I adapted an article from Kathleen Martin and James Garrett to show Indigenous (Native American)

TABLE 3.2 Indigenous spaces in school

This activity will help educators link school space to inclusivity and exclusivity in current research.

INDIGENOUS DAKOTA CULTURAL PRACTICE
Storytelling as a means of learning, confirming reality, preserving community, and conveying knowledge. Storytelling preserves Indigenous Dakota space.

Exclusionary school response:	*Inclusionary* school response:
Establishing a storytelling club or inviting an Indian "storyteller" into school to tell "stories," perhaps around Thanksgiving.	Including storytelling as central to all learning practices in the school—for all students, Indigenous and non-Indigenous.

Leadership role:
Leadership team should recognize space as being connected to how knowledge is preserved and shared, and should work to institutionalize storytelling—*as well as the knowledge contained in the narratives*—throughout curriculum, policy making, and leadership practice.

INDIGENOUS DAKOTA CULTURAL PRACTICE
Communal learning as a way of affirming Indigenous epistemology, existence, and space.

Exclusionary school response:	*Inclusionary* school response:
Reliance on testing systems to "measure" knowledge and to have students compete with one another (i.e., which individuals have the highest test scores).	As a way of "learning by doing," have students work together on all assessment tasks to complement each other's knowledge (and offset any perceived gaps in knowledge).

Leadership role:
The leadership team should establish communal learning—and not comparison/competition-based standardized testing—as standard throughout the curriculum. This communal learning can look different in different places, but in Dakota space, it should always include (a) learning in connection with other human beings (especially elders) and (b) a connection with the communities in which students live.

INDIGENOUS DAKOTA CULTURAL PRACTICE
Connecting lived surroundings with lived experiences as a way of existing in Dakota space.

Exclusionary school response:	*Inclusionary* school response:
Teaching and learning about environmental pollution in earth science or biology classes.	Including the preservation of community and land as the primary goal of schooling and all learning activities; this—and not high test scores, successful college careers, or even employment—should serve as the primary goal for learning.

continues

TABLE 3.2 *Continued*

Leadership role:
Using school budget and resources to extend community-based (not White/Western) service-learning opportunities that allow students to preserve Indigenous land and the environment.

INDIGENOUS DAKOTA CULTURAL PRACTICE
Centering knowledge from elders as a way to understand oneself, the community, and the broader world, as well as pass down intergenerational tradition and knowledge.

Exclusionary school response:	*Inclusionary* school response:
Contacting parents when there is a perceived problem with their children; or, minstrelizing or tokenizing elders by bringing them in to tell exotic stories about the tribe.	Recognizing the "circle of knowledge"; also recognizing that elders and parents are preservers and maintainers of knowledge, and that this knowledge is equally—if not more—valid than the scientific knowledge that is celebrated in most public schools. Thus, this knowledge must flow into multiple teaching and policy-making spaces in the school.

Leadership role:
Leadership team should recognize that Indigenous Dakota space must have elders—their wisdom, knowledge, behaviors, and epistemologies must be a permanent fixture in all learning spaces. Given this reality, leadership teams must bring elders and parents onto the staff into regular (not only "cultural") staff positions.

Dakota "space" as inclusionary (honored, celebrated, and incorporated) or exclusionary (contained, pushed away, or unwelcomed) in school.[6] Frameworks and examples like this should be developed for every unique minoritized community served in your school. Remember, "space" here includes not only a physical space, but also *everything* even associated with that space—imagined or real.

LEADERSHIP AND EXCLUSIONARY PRACTICES IN DAVISTOWN

Minoritized students in Davistown were many times more likely than their White peers to be suspended or excluded from school, to drop out of school, to receive worse grades, and to perform worse on standardized achievement tests. The rates were especially egregious for Black students, and particularly Black males; in some instances, they were more than twenty times more likely to be suspended than their White classmates for the same offenses. This was not the case at UAHS. Joe insisted that suspensions were not helpful for students, and in my two years in the school as a researcher, I counted less than a handful of suspensions.

Exclusionary practices were rife in Davistown. But researchers have also noted the power that school leaders can have on whether exclusionary practices are institutionalized or challenged.[7] As Brown states, "The notion that school administration is neutral in application for educating children of all races and ethnicities fails to consider disparities in political power between racial groups."[8] Similarly, Lomotey explains that "the leadership of the principal affects the behavior of the teachers which subsequently affects the achievement of students: Focus on the impact that the leadership of the principal has on aspects of the school environment."[9] In other words, culturally responsive school leadership requires a nuanced perspective that acknowledges power and privilege. And CRSL can have impact! So, in addition to considering the community perspectives (chapter 1) and being self-reflective (chapter 2), culturally responsive principals assume an anti-oppressive posture when they are confronted with exclusionary programmatic or pedagogical practices in school. *More often than not, the principal is directly responsible for oversight of the oppressive practice and has the power to confront and push back against it.* In Davistown, the principal chose to critique and challenge exclusionary practices present in the district.

Between Student Disengagement and Critical Self-Reflection

And if I pressure 'em and say, "What's going on? Why are you not working?" then they just give you a wall [blank face] and they don't—they don't share anything. Academically, I don't really push hard on the kids, I kinda back off and then encourage 'em. If they're having a bad day, then they're having a bad day. I can't expect everyone to respond every single day.

—MELISSA, UAHS science teacher

When I began my teaching career in Detroit, it was common for me to hear comments similar to this one made by Melissa. Melissa's position, that she doesn't want to pressure students who are "having a bad day," suggests that she was contributing to student disengagement. Even more alarming, she likely thought she was being kind or loving to those students. This, in effect, would serve to *fossilize* her into maintaining low expectations for her Black, Latinx, and other minoritized students. When UAHS students appeared to disengage, she was not culturally responsive in at least two ways: One, she assumed that she, or her teaching, had no role in the disengagement—this is a wielding of power (i.e., the power to determine the meaning and presence of disengagement). And two, she allowed what she perceived as "student disengagement" to happen.

But researchers widely agree that allowing students to withdraw from classroom learning—that is, by acquiescing to student disengagement—is hurtful to the student in many ways.[10] In particular, this lowering of expectations is another harmful but less noticed way of school exclusion. Students academically and behaviorally disengage from education because it is a solution for them, not a problem.[11] Thus, what teachers have long interpreted as "disengagement" may have been resistance to hostile classroom environments or curricula. To be sure, students who have been facing exclusionary climates for years—for example, forms of anti-Blackness, epistemicide of Indigenous knowledge, homophobia, or Islamophobia—actually have reasons for disengaging from environments they perceive to be violent and hostile. After all, how could any reasonable educator expect students to repeatedly and consistently expose their psychological and emotional selves to forms of hostility, abuse, or violence? Would any educator remain in such contexts, in hopes of promises often not fulfilled or for benefits that seem so distant? Studies have shown that some of the brightest students have *chosen* to disengage from and/or leave school (i.e., school pushouts).

Melissa's anecdote likely referred to her experiences with Selena, an eleventh-grade Latina student in her class. Selena was a first-generation Mexican student who came to the United States with her parents when she was three years old. Melissa had frequently given Selena permission to leave her classroom during times of instruction. In the week that I interviewed Selena, I counted that she twice visited other classrooms for ESL services during times of instruction. She also visited the counselor once, the social worker once, another teacher's classroom twice, and the administrator's office once. Melissa did not notice a pattern, but Joe did, and mentioned it to Melissa: "I've see her outside of your classroom a few times this week already, and we've just got to have the kids in our classroom, or they're not going to learn." I asked Selena, who seemed to speak English like a native speaker, why she kept leaving Melissa's classroom. She attributed it directly to her comfort level and interest in Melissa's class: "Cause that's like my least favorite class. And she don't really care, she just lets me leave the class. But I'm still getting an A in her class. I know I shouldn't though. But, like my other teachers, like, what they teach is related to me, but it's just hard for her to do that. I don't like science like that. And my friends are in Mr. Hope's [ESL] class."

It is important for us to put Selena's "disengagement" into proper context. Indeed, Selena's response was an indictment of Melissa's teaching and classroom content. Despite the fact that science and math teaching can be culturally responsive to students, Selena saw no relevance in Melissa's class and constantly found reasons to leave it.[12] It is troubling that some teachers may not realize that they have lowered expectations for some students. Chunn found that "academic sorting practices and their selective determinants, teachers' expectations, and race and socioeconomic status influence black students' scholastic success or failure."[13] At UAHS, it is not that Selena and other minoritized students all came from "broken" homes and just decided to disengage from class one day. They made informed decisions because of the classroom climates and/or pedagogies they experienced. Selena was making a decision to remove herself from Melissa's class.

Deal Making: Lowering Expectations of Minoritized Youth

The disengagement that teachers allowed—and in some cases, facilitated—happened at UAHS is multiple ways. Some teachers at UAHS allowed students to disengage because of fear of conflict with students or classroom disruptions; this type of deal making between students and harmony-seeking teachers is common.[14] Incidents of deal making typically allow students to engage in non-academic activities (e.g., drawing, resting the head on a desk, using small electronics, or playing a game with another disengaged student), and in exchange, students may be quieter or less challenging to teachers. Like other researchers, I argue that deal making results from teachers' fear of being unable to control their classrooms, or from low expectations of minoritized students, which results in temporary teacher comfort or classroom harmony.[15] Since the principal often challenged the practice of teachers allowing students to physically leave their academic classes, some UAHS teachers resorted to a classroom-based deal-making (exclusionary) practice. But this type of bargaining also has a negative academic impact on students.[16] In one instance, a UAHS math teacher rationalized the preference of her own harmony over that of the students' long-term academic interests:

> When I really pushed, in the beginning when I got here, I pushed too hard, I really got resentment. So now when I just back off and say, "Okay, here's the assignment today," and they'll say, "I don't feel like it!" I don't respond, I don't challenge them. 'Cause it's like, what for? I'm gonna get chaos, I'm gonna disturb the rest of the class, for what?
>
> —JESSICA, UAHS math teacher

This comment from Jessica, a White teacher with over fifteen years of teaching experience, confirms teacher facilitation of student disengagement. Many of the stereotypes that the teacher held of her students, most of whom were Black and Latinx, came into focus as the teacher rationalized her decision not to hold high academic standards for students of color. These minoritized students had experienced years of exclusionary pressures and the trauma of removal from the schools in the district, as had their family members in prior generations. And now, they were experiencing a softer type of bigotry. While some researchers have demonstrated the pervasive tendency of White teachers to lower expectations for Black students, I argue in this book that all teachers, including White teachers, must maintain high expectations of minoritized students.[17] And if they do not, it is the principals' responsibility—regardless of the leader's race, or their fear of unions, or their fear of pushback from racial discussions, or other hurdles—to challenge the exclusionary practice of lowering inter- and intra-classroom-based academic expectations. In the next section, I discuss some of the responsibilities of culturally responsive school leaders in responding to (a) what appears to be student disengagement, and (b) low teacher expectations of minoritized students.

CRSL Response to Low Teacher Expectations

My research suggests two overarching, culturally responsive ways that principals can respond to exclusionary practices. First, culturally responsive school principals can mentor teachers in being inclusionary and model these inclusionary behaviors themselves; if needed, principals can then challenge exclusionary behaviors of teachers and other staff. During the course of this study, Joe demonstrated these three behaviors with Melissa, Jessica, and other staff members displaying exclusionary practices—such as teacher requests of student suspension, sending students to other classes during instructional time, and in-class deal making, to name just a few. Second, culturally responsive school principals can build inclusionary capacity in partnership with parents and students. So at UAHS, stereotypes about minoritized student space could not be used as an excuse for exclusionary practices in the school space.

Moreover, Joe was able to establish a culture that promoted student and parent perspectives as an inclusionary voice. He did this by establishing a practice whereby students and parents became self-advocates. The principal was not only courageous enough to listen to these voices, but he encouraged students and their families to be self-advocates for inclusionary practices (e.g., for their own presence in schools, both personally and for minoritized cultures). Whether in personal conferences with families and teachers, in rap sessions, or in staff meetings, Joe judiciously positioned student and family voices not with suspicion, but as truth. I discuss these approaches next.

LEADING INCLUSIVENESS IN SCHOOL

It is crucial that we understand a recurring point throughout this book: researchers have found that *school principals* (and other building administrators) are best positioned to resist oppressive practices in the building. This happens in multiple ways. Here, I focus on how CRSL principals build organizational capacity. At UAHS, this happened by establishing mentoring relationships, modeling, challenging exclusionary practices, and fostering self-advocacy skills in children. It also happened through school training and professional development, but I take that up extensively in chapter 5.

Mentoring

When culturally responsive school principals encounter exclusionary practices among their teachers, they should begin by mentoring teachers in being inclusionary with minoritized students, families, and cultures.[18] At UAHS, mentoring consisted of Joe or other inclusionary staff having open discourse about how they were "being fair with the kids." This open discourse allowed Joe, the UAHS social worker, the community liaison, and a host of other mentor teachers to help teachers become more inclusive. Here is a list of elements of CRSL mentoring as it happened at UAHS:

- *Open discourse.* Joe and all of his teachers had both private and open discussions about what they could do better to serve the UAHS students, and how they could be more fair. Rap sessions were one way this work happened; staff meetings were another. Joe would ask staff directly, "Since kicking kids out or allowing the kids to leave your classroom harms them, what can you do to keep the kids in your classroom?" This encouraged conversations about inclusion and exclusion to be ongoing and connected to practice.
- *Mentoring partnerships.* In some instances, Joe would ask inclusionary teachers to help other teachers who had poor classroom management and who displayed exclusionary practices.
- *Personal mentoring relationships.* Joe established relationships with some exclusionary teachers in which he personally encouraged them to see how their exclusionary decisions would negatively impact students and their opportunities.

Modeling

While many researchers and practitioners have described formal modeling structures in schools and organization, the modeling at UAHS happened in very public and informal ways.[19] In rap sessions, Joe would have public dialogues with students who felt marginalized and voiceless. Students were encouraged to express if they felt they were being treated unfairly, and some were comfortable doing so. Some students publicly critiqued Joe during these sessions, and he modeled for UAHS staff how students and parents were to have their voices heard, honored, and responded to. At times, he disagreed with the parent or student perspectives, and after entering conversation, they often came to a negotiated agreement about what happened and what should be done. I asked Joe about his role in conveying and demonstrating anti-oppressive and inclusionary practices to colleagues, and he remarked, "You've got to lead by example, so I use every opportunity to demonstrate that every kid belongs here, every day." From Joe's example and other instances of CRSL, I pull the following elements:

- Modeling inclusionary practices should happen in *public* (i.e., schoolwide) conversations. There should be public affirmations that all minoritized students and their families are welcomed and valued in school.
- Modeling should happen *at the moment* that principals observe or encounter oppressive exclusionary requests or behaviors from staff.
- Modeling should also happen in direct private interactions that families have with Joe. Teachers often "sat in" on such conversations when Joe sought moments of community perspective and voice.

A Need for Courage: Challenging Exclusionary Practice

When mentoring, modeling, training, personal conversations, and private and public discussions failed to dissuade UAHS staff from exclusionary behaviors, Joe directly challenged individual staff members. It was also common for him to challenge the entire staff. Any indications of exclusionary behaviors toward children were not allowed. When several teachers described Joe as "not having any backbone" and said that "he is now way more weak than he used to be because he won't kick the kids out anymore," it became apparent that the exclusionary practices could be halted by a culturally responsive school leader, even when teachers appeared to resist or to resent more inclusionary actions. In one instance, Joe challenged an African American English teacher to "stop chiding and shaming the kids for who they are!" In other instances, he would question and critique teachers who pushed students out of their classrooms or simply let the students leave.

I have shared examples of this throughout this text, but school leaders who seek to be culturally responsible should remember the importance of trust. Challenging teachers can cause anxiety for both leaders and educators, and can diminish trust and positive culture in buildings; it may not be best to *begin* with challenging teachers, because mentoring and modeling often work so well. Thus it's important to note that to challenge teachers with whom the leader has not developed trusting relationships can cause more harm than good to the principal-teacher relationship. Joe had the trust of teachers as well as students and community.

Fostering Self-Advocacy:
Supporting Student Self-Reflection and Emancipation

According to current research, self-advocacy skills can help empower marginalized students. This does *not* mean that the onus of anti-oppressive work in schools rests on the shoulders of students or parents. But it does mean that they can and should be partners in this work. Traditional self-advocacy approaches used in special education impart to students four key skills: increasing students' knowledge about their disability, helping students (and their families) understand the services for which they qualify, helping students understand their rights under the law, and helping students to become aware of their educational and social opportunities and expectations.[20] In a slight modification of this prior research, I reshape self-advocacy theory by allowing it to address the needs of minoritized students, and imparting tools that support children and families in their own struggles for justice and space in school. This modified version of self-advocacy theory aims to:

- Increase students' (and their families') knowledge about how traditional schools may have marginalized them, their families, and their communities.
- Help students understand how they may use school resources because they have been underserved—for example, if they attend a school with low standardized test scores. (I am not endorsing such tests, but suggesting that resources may be available because of them.)
- Help students understand their legal and educational rights (e.g., their rights for inclusion in school, legally and culturally).
- Help students understand the educational and social opportunities they are entitled to (e.g., social capital exchanges previously open only to upperclass White students).
- Help students understand how they can position their presence, voice, and interests in all aspects of schooling and learning.

Joe fostered these skills by posing questions to students and their families that helped guide a discourse that challenged exclusionary practices. As discussed above, exclusionary practices are not static—though equally destructive, they can be direct or less direct, and as with all other forms of oppression, they constantly shape and maintain privilege for those with power. Joe would frequently ask students and parents, "Why do you deserve to be here?" During a school intake interview, Joe spoke with Marcus, a new eighth-grade student, as his mother, Bertha, added her thoughts:

JOE: Why do you think you deserve to be here at this school?

MARCUS: I don't know; I just heard good things about this school. That, like, they be treatin' students fair, and don't be trying to find reasons to put students out. And that it's just funner.

JOE: Well, that tells me about the school, but what about you: What is it about you that makes you deserve to be here?

MARCUS: I'm ready to change, like I wanna graduate. I feel like the other schools don't want me there, but I should have the opportunity to get right and graduate.

BERTHA: Yeah, it's like the other schools don't want us there even for those students who be trying to do right. I done had enough of it.

JOE: Okay, well, you gonna encounter some of that here too. But what you just told me, you need to tell them too, if you should ever encounter that kinda bullshit.

Yet, self-advocacy runs the risk of positioning "anti-oppressive education" as the responsibility of students to bear the brunt of resisting their own oppression. This is unfairly taxing on minoritized students, and in reality, it's everyone's responsibility—primarily educators'. However, at UAHS, student self-advocacy was a powerful tool used in resistance to teachers' exclusionary practices.

Mentoring, modeling, and challenging oppression when confronted were all inclusionary leadership responses that Joe directed toward exclusionary UAHS staff. In addition, fostering student self-advocacy and a sense of belonging in school was a leadership behavior Joe utilized to center community-based epistemologies in school

FIGURE 3.1 Activity (15–30 days): Sharing space

Principal should form a group with parents, teachers, administrators, and students. Reserve space for parents and students who are not often engaged with the school. Ask the group to repurpose the school space in ways that benefit the neighborhood community. Conduct research to find out the most pressing needs for residents, children, parents, and leaders in the community. Ask the group to write a proposal for using school resources and school space to "host" the community's needs.

Principal's Task

Seek to establish policy-making contributions from this group by asking minoritized parents to contribute to crafting school or district policy.

Superintendent's Task (once every thirty days)

Visit the homes of minoritized families to hear their experiences of schools and their community-based concerns.

leadership practice for minoritized students. This aspect of CRSL was not limited to the centering of epistemologies of marginalized people and communities. It included consistent practices that pushed staff to identify and challenge behaviors that were dismissive or even oppressive toward students and families. If done consistently, the activities in figure 3.1 should help leaders stay informed about how to promote inclusive spaces in school.

CONCLUSION

In this chapter, I discussed how schools provide either exclusionary or inclusionary spaces for minoritized youth. A constant theme throughout this book has been the reproductive nature of educational practices in schools. To be sure, teachers and leaders do not have to do much—literally, nothing—for exclusionary (i.e., oppressive) practices to be reproduced. I have argued in this chapter that school leaders—because of their higher levels of power and privilege—are best positioned to either protect or challenge the oppression. In this conclusion, I share a few reflections on the data connected with school inclusion. The inclusionary school climate at UAHS caused the students to feel a strong sense of belonging, which improved the enrollment and attendance for minoritized students, who often felt unwelcomed in their previous school. But this "sense of belonging" is only a result of students' and parents' perception that the principal and teachers went out of their way to promote an inclusive space for them, and were willing to fight for them to be in school. The students received this message from the school, and responded by coming and excelling in school.

Diverse, Intergenerational Communities

Community epistemology and voice is itself diverse across gender, race, income, education, and level of resistance/passivity, among other things. And some voices are certainly more powerful and more heard than others. Educators and administrators understand that there are differences within a community, but without deep knowledge of a community, they often reproduce power inequities within the communities they serve. Here is an example to demonstrate what I mean.

I remember visiting a district in Minnesota with a large refugee population. After visiting with the superintendent and key staff, I met with the community representatives in the district. I learned there were some dominant groups/tribes within a particular refugee population, including tribes that were more established in the city that housed this district. After doing some intense community outreach, the district hired a person from this refugee community as a liaison, who then helped to guide the district into hiring additional staff. Unfortunately, the additional hires were all of a single clan. The other clans were intentionally kept from the district leadership, their needs were not met, and their children were not served well. Unknowingly, the district had perpetuated inequities among some of its students. From the district's vantage point, however, it had established relationships with this entire refugee community. Yet there is neither a monolithic nor a representative community voice; rather, it is constantly contested, negotiated, and shared among multiple communities.

It is important to note that community voice is also intergenerational. Across the data for UAHS, the voices of grandparents, parents, aunts, uncles, and children converged to express community perspectives, but it also became clear that community voice is contested and dynamic. Children as young as thirteen years old would partake in conversations with their parents and other community members within and outside of schools. Any topic was allowed: how schooling should happen, how students are treated, and whether they felt a connection to school. This was a powerful way of sharing a diverse, contested community voice that was used to shape UAHS policy; students, parents, and elderly all shared in an open, impactful way. Ancestral, community-based, and "old school" knowledge was passed down as students' hip-hop knowledge was passed up; this tension was useful for schools and liberatory for students and communities.

But What About "Behavior Modification"?

He's like a grandfather. When they're [students] down he wants to figure out, [For example, Joe may ask:] "Why you got an attitude today? . . . If you done crapped on yourself, you better come tell me." He wants to help.

—DARNELL, former UAHS student

By now, I hope it is clear that principals are the gatekeepers (i.e., the most important person in a school) who can either prevent or perpetuate the school-to-prison-pipeline. My practitioner colleagues often have a central question for me: Are you saying that anything goes at UAHS; is there no attempt to modify behaviors? Answering this question requires precision because many student behaviors seen as "deviant" are actually not and are simply socially constructed;

schools often serve to protect behaviors common of White students while shaming, policing, or punishing behaviors associated with Indigenous, Black, and Latinx students.

But there are some behaviors that Joe actually did find to be detrimental to students—such as drug use, all forms of criminal acts that were punishable by law, tardiness and truancy, fighting, and irresponsible sexual habits. He regularly engaged in leadership practices through which he would attempt to modify student behaviors that he thought to be poor choices. Mostly, he would have open conversations with students about their behaviors and how they felt about them, and how they had grown in these areas. These conversations happened in private as well as in schoolwide venues.

Because the established relationships between Joe and students were built on trust and mutual respect, students said they were comfortable with Joe pushing them on some of their behaviors. Joe set a tone for a school culture that prevented negative imagery and ridicule of students, including those who wanted to succeed socially and academically; in this way, students were able to perform well while maintaining their dignity and their urban identities. The principal promoted a school environment where students redefined themselves in a psychologically safe and dignified manner. Joe's comment—"If you done crapped on yourself, you better come tell me"—suggests that he believed they could improve, and that he encouraged them to change. Figure 3.2 indicates a consistent yet dynamic process through

FIGURE 3.2 Community-based behavioral modification

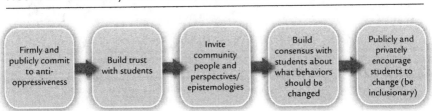

which Joe would encourage behaviors that he felt would contribute to school success.

Advocacy Leadership with Community: Toward Inclusionary School Space

Culturally responsive school leadership must advocate for what is in the best interests of the community. This could mean the principal advocates for causes like fair, affordable housing and the protection of immigrant rights, or against crime, joblessness, or mass incarceration targeting Black men. Every principal and school leader should advocate for a cause that is connected with and important to the community. But principals and other school leaders must also advocate against exclusionary practices such as shaming minoritized students because of their culture; privileging Euro-American behaviors or behaviors common to White students; and minoritizing through suspensions, expulsions, and school push-out practices. Scholars have demonstrated that parents and school staff should collaborate with schools to advocate for marginalized children.[21] This research challenges portrayals of marginalized parents as passive recipients of educators' social justice efforts; rather, it looks at the active roles they can play, and at how principals can help develop these parents and students as *self-advocates*. But it is also true that educators cannot place the work of anti-oppressive and inclusionary schooling on parents and students. There will be tension, but the best approach is for this to be a collaborative effort, with community knowledge and epistemology guiding the process.

CHAPTER 3

Discussion Questions

For Principals

1. Identify and examine three pieces of direct exclusionary practice data and three pieces of less-direct exclusionary practice data in your school. Which staff members are most responsible for reproducing these practices?

2. How do you incorporate parents' and community's understandings into leadership behaviors?

3. How is your school constructed in the community's recent and distant memory? How would different minoritized community members describe the inclusiveness of the school?

For Teacher Leaders and Equity Leadership Team

1. How does your team regularly monitor the incidents of exclusionary practices in the school?

2. How do you mentor the staff members most responsible for the school's exclusionary practices for minoritized students?

For Superintendents and District Office Staff

1. What resources are given to schools to combat exclusionary practices?

2. How could you disincentivize or discourage exclusionary practices in school? Where could you pull resources from to fund this work?

"I DON'T CARE WHO YOU SAY YOU ARE! CAN YOU LEARN?!"

Identity Confluence and the Humanization of Minoritized Youth Identity

Even today, so brainwashed is this republic that people seriously ask in what they suppose to be good faith, "what does the Negro want?" I've heard a great many asinine question is my life, but that is perhaps the most asinine and perhaps the most insulting. But the point here is that people who ask the question, thinking that they ask in good faith, are really the victims of this conspiracy to make Negroes believe they are less than human . . . I began by saying that one of the paradoxes of education was that precisely at the point when you begin to develop a conscience, you must find yourself at war with your society.

—JAMES BALDWIN[1]

Today, I want to talk with you all about your future plans. We've been focusing on this because some of you were unsure about what you wanted to do with your lives before coming to this school. Now, who wants to go to college? [All students in the school raise their hands.] Well, if you want to go to college, we want to help you. But let us know how we can help you. What do we need to help you with to make you successful, so that you can have the academic skills needed for college?

—JOE, UAHS principal

Joe's words here lead me to begin this chapter with two reminders. First, as educators attempt to regulate student identity (via policing, containment, reform, shame, etc.), we must be careful not to continue the historically oppressive treatment of minoritized communities and students in school. Second, students will not change who they are for us, and if they see the choice as changing or quitting, they often make informed decisions to leave school (i.e., to drop out). When Joe asked his students, "Who wants to go to college?," he highlighted two important leadership behaviors: acceptance of Indigenous student identity and encouragement of an "academic student identity." In chapter 3, I argued that culturally responsive school leaders promote inclusion of community-based epistemologies and that there are several CRSL behaviors that can resist exclusionary school contexts. But as a teacher in Detroit, I quickly learned that marginalization was not simply about physically removing students from school. In fact, the disparagement of students who were always in school and never suspended was often even more troubling and was as violent as the exclusionary practices outlined in the last chapter.

In this chapter, I argue for ways that culturally responsive school leaders can embrace the expressions of student identities and voices that are most often marginalized within schools. Through a process I call *identity confluence,* I present data that suggests students' academic identities are developed alongside local Indigenous identities that typically are pushed out of school. Here the seminal works of Mehan, Hubbard, and Villanueva as well as my own research are important.[2] I also use the work of González, Moll, and Amanti, who argue that "people are competent, they have knowledge, and their life experiences have given them that knowledge . . . firsthand research experiences [that educators conduct] with families allow one to document this competence and knowledge."[3] These authors propose that all students draw from unique *funds of knowledge.* But for us, Indigenous or community-based knowledge is not only used to improve the curriculum and teacher knowledge; it can also be used at an administrative level to shape policy and the humanization of minoritized students throughout the school.

I also refer to concepts of *cultural* and *social capital,* which I explain later in the chapter. The UAHS school leader not only embraced the local Indigenous identities, but he valued the identities by engaging and advocating for them. Thus, I shall principally argue that all student identities should be welcomed in school, and that culturally responsive principals promote a school environment that protects these identities. Based on the data I present, I further argue that students need academic identities (that is, identities in which they feel smart and capable, and that provide a sense of academic belonging) and encouragement toward improving behaviors, but this attempt to improve their behaviors should never be done at the expense of their community-based, Indigenous identities. In other words, their access to power should never be accessible only if they are asked to give up something that White students are allowed to keep.

Throughout this chapter, I connect student identity with the concept of humanization. In discussing its meaning, I briefly reflect on the colonization and enslavement of minoritized and Indigenous people. While Indigenous bodies, minds, lands, and resources were crucial for the accumulations of White/Western wealth, it is also noteworthy that the criminalization and containment (both material and epistemological) of non-White communities were among the most blatant tactics used. Why is this important to the field of education and school leadership? Unfortunately, current forms of dehumanization—containment, criminalization, decentering, deficitizing, and so on—within schools are outgrowths of these earlier forms of oppression. But I present data that suggests that school leaders and teachers can be humanizing to minoritized students. In the UAHS example, this meant that the leaders could promote environments and institutionalize practices that would both humanize minoritized student identities and encourage academic identities. That happened in two distinct ways: (1) by establishing social and educational networks that were beneficial to minoritized students, families, communities, and teachers; and (2) by using community-based (ancestral) knowledge to help teachers understand and appreciate minoritized student identities. And finally, many of the examples that I share are meant to challenge the conventional thinking of school leaders and urge them to consider what *can* work for them. Indeed, there are many cultures, and cultures are nonstatic and dynamic, and schools are all structured differently. The main takeaways from this research, however, can be used to push staffs into discussions that will lead to more equitable learning for all students.

SUPPORTING INDIGENOUS AND MINORITIZED STUDENT IDENTITIES: THE ROLE OF LEADERS?

It is important to note again that school leaders are in the critical position of having the power to directly address systems of oppression, such as the school-to-prison pipeline. At UAHS, the principal put structures in place that humanized and normalized minoritized student identities. Culturally responsive school leaders have access to power, and they can use their power to give greater access, belongingness, and opportunity to minoritized students and families. Lisa Delpit describes a "culture of power" and how some groups gain access to power. In her view, there are rules for participating in the culture of power that "relate to linguistic forms, communicative strategies, and presentation of self; that is, ways of talking, ways of writing, ways of dressing, and ways of interacting."[4] Joe, students, staff, and parents had an ongoing discourse about how identities must be allowed to exist in school "without feeling like they're unwelcome here, because everybody is welcome." Whether in rap sessions or private conferences, parents pushed students and staff to be more inclusive, and students pushed their parents and teachers. The driving question that Joe asked students was: "Can you learn?" Though posed to students, it was also a challenge to teachers who wished to ostracize some student identities. His message to teachers was more pointed: "I know some of you may have problematic perceptions of our students and who they claim to be, but you cannot dehuman-ize them for that—be it through shaming, criminalizing, excluding, or other practices." To students, the question meant: "Despite all of your other interests, will you commit to seeing yourself as dedicated to academic success if we create an environment where you feel safe and dignified, and experience a sense of belonging?"

Minoritized students were accustomed to having their voices and identities silenced in traditional schools in Davistown. In an interview with one of the traditional high school principals in the district, he talked about a "White Jewish girl" who was heavily im-mersed in volunteerism and civic student activities. He praised the girl and said that she had a 4.0 grade point average, but that Black students "don't know how to play the game," and that they never participated in any activities like these (the school and district were in an area that had three major hospitals and several large universi-ties, and hence had a great number of volunteer and civic activities; volunteerism was socially rewarded in this locale). From this princi-pal's statement, it seemed that he socially rewarded this White stu-dent for her volunteer and extracurricular activities. It also seemed he blamed Black students for being "uninvolved." Most unfortunate, this Black principal was hired to better serve the Black students and families in the district. But he seemed to have no awareness of the cultural wealth that the Black students and families brought to his school, and the data at this school—which showed that Black stu-dents were more than twenty times more likely than White students to be suspended for the same behaviors—bore this out.

The UAHS experience was quite different for Black and other minoritized students; the principal did not dehumanize or crim-inalize Black student identities, and he challenged staff who attempted to do so. At UAHS, hip-hop dress, language, and man-nerisms were common. I asked Harold, a White teacher who taught technology at UAHS, about the inclusion of Black student identity, and he responded:

> I think that our culture at [UAHS] mirrors more of the African American culture in the community than it does the Caucasian society . . . And I think that it just helps the kids feel comfortable when they come here 'cause that's what they're used to. And they go to the big schools, they don't have anybody, they don't feel like they have anybody they can relate to or is relating with them in the larger schools, and they [educators at the other schools] just want them to assimilate to dominant culture and ignore their own, the kids' culture that . . . just helps them feel connected. And our kids, kids in general, adults in general, aren't gonna admit that they don't know something to someone they don't trust, and so our kids never made a connection in the larger schools.

Harold's response signals a type of White insecurity and fragility in his perception that Black identities are becoming more prominent. He described a culture that embraces minoritized identities in the school. This is important, because in recent research, scholars have argued that it is actually more humanizing and culturally responsive for all students (including White students) to have Indigenous epistemologies and ancestral knowledge[5] at the center of school curriculum and pedagogy.[6] In table 4.1, I offer examples of useful ways to recognize behaviors as being humanized and conflated with good academic behaviors. School leaders must be more vigilant in ensuring that student behaviors are attached to identity. When teachers punish minoritized cultural behaviors while normalizing behaviors common to White students, they are assaulting community-based and Indigenous identities. After humanizing and embracing minoritized students and their behaviors—and preventing the shaming, teasing, or suppression of student identities—CRSL principals find ways

TABLE 4.1 Examples of student behaviors and teacher responses

Student behavior	Examples of teacher responses		
	Dehumanizing	Humanizing	Identity confluence for academic identity
Student dances to hip-hop music in the classroom.	Teacher jokes about dancing and compares student to a popular performer.	Teacher thanks student for display of cultural practices.	Teacher approaches students and parents for help with including hip-hop as a common theme throughout the curriculum.
Student speaks a language other than English during the lesson.	Teacher complains to administrator and parents about language use in the classroom, claiming that students need to learn English to be successful in class.	Teacher looks for community volunteers who can facilitate dual language (and culture) usage in the classroom.	Teacher allows students to use their native language whenever they want—including during some learning activities—but also teaches students proper use of English.
Student wears a Black Lives Matter T-shirt.	Teacher criticizes student for wearing the shirt and claims student is being provocative or divisive.	Teacher thanks student for bringing the perspective into the class.	Teacher asks the student in private if he or she is willing to co-lead a lesson on the topic on the shirt; if not, could the student identify a community member who could do so.
Student refuses to comply with a teacher's request about standing up only when given permission.	Teacher writes a disciplinary referral and sends the student to the principal's office for "insubordination" or "disrespect."	Teacher explains the objective of the rule and asks for the student's perspective. Teacher asks if teacher and student can help each other reach respective goals.	Teacher and student come to a mutual understanding about standing in class, which ends up allowing students to stand whenever they like to complete assignments.

to add or encourage academic identities. In other words, only after principals have actually humanized student identities can we begin to focus on developing academic identities, learning behaviors, aspects of curriculum, and school structures that would contribute to student success.

But what are specific *culturally responsive school leadership behaviors* that both humanize student identities and promote academic identities in minoritized youth? Indeed, not all student behaviors are cultural in nature. In most schools, final decisions about student removal or acceptance rest with school leaders. In addition to promoting inclusive practices, leadership teams can center student voice, and use this voice as data to determine the extent to which school environments are welcoming toward children. At UAHS, Joe promoted an environment that humanized minoritized student identities and promoted academic identities in two distinct ways: (1) he established social and educational networks that were beneficial to minoritized students, families, and communities (social capital), and (2) he used community-based (ancestral) knowledge to help teachers understand and appreciate minoritized student identities (funds of knowledge and cultural capital).

SOCIAL CAPITAL IN SUPPORT OF MINORITIZED AND INDIGENOUS STUDENT IDENTITIES

Student *social capital* is when students or their families have relationships or are a part of networks that end up being educationally or socially beneficial to them. Scholars have found that Black, Brown, Latinx, and other minoritized students have social capital that is not valued in traditional schools.[7] Morgan and Sørensen show that social capital is contextualized; they illustrate how different types of social capital may be present in different situations, which may be positive in some cases, yet negative or exclusionary in others.[8] For Black students in Davistown's traditional schools, social capital was un-recognized, neglected, or unconnected to power that led to tangible benefits for minoritized students. In other words, minoritized families received no social capital benefits despite "relationships" with people with (and in) power. Resources and information that would help their children were not shared with them. In Davistown, traditional schools tended to privilege families that had power, access, and special privileges.

The traditional school principals in Davistown did not know how to establish positive relationships with minoritized families, and most certainly had no skill in connecting minoritized families to networks that would benefit their children. The problem was particularly egregious for Black parents and students. All of the Black parents and students interviewed for this study felt that traditional school leaders and educators were exclusionary toward their children because of how the educators generally viewed Black students. In an interview with a parent about her daughter, who was not a student at UAHS, Tersa, captured this point: "They always associated my daughter, and all of the Black kids, with being ghetto, and then they treat us bad. And many of us are educated, but it doesn't matter. And it shouldn't matter anyway, but it is not right that they cannot see the diversity." According to this woman, other parents often complained to her about the harsh treatment of Black students in the district's traditional schools.

She further complained that "privileged" information never reached her or other Black parents in the district, even though she was an extremely active parent. She gave the example of discovering that college courses were being offered at her daughter's middle school—but no notice had been given to her. She described how many of her close White associates—whose children were current enrollees of the college credit program—never mentioned it to her or other Black parents. Since no formal notice went to the homes of parents, she felt that she and her daughter had been both socially and academically excluded from this opportunity. So while Black parents did have social capital with each other, the *power* and *benefits* connected to White parents' capital did not extend to that Black network. At UAHS, Joe pushed back against a culture of exclusionary networks by establishing networks that (a) were inclusive of minoritized families and (b) had access to resources that were beneficial to minoritized students.

Establishing Social Capital Networks for Minoritized Families

Here, I share what worked for folks at UAHS. But school staff should work with the community to craft goals of expanding parental social capital within their own local contexts. Cultivating relationships among parents—and their connection to school personnel—is one way social capital was established in Davistown. Joe repeatedly asked parents to inform him of what was going on in the community so that he could raise concerns to the district's board of education or bodies with power. He also promoted relationships and networks within the school itself (meaning school staff, activities, spaces, resources) and forged the necessary relationships with parents to ensure the children's success. More importantly, he held school activities where parents passed on information about opportunities between themselves. This information was shared among parents during events that Joe designed. In fact, there were a number of noteworthy tactics instrumental in accommodating and facilitating social capital between parents and school staff at UAHS:

- *NAAPID (National African American Parent Involvement Day).* NAAPID has become a widely celebrated event that occurs annually on the second Monday of February. Cities across the country partake in the event, which encourages African American parents to go to their child's school. The NAAPID event reinforces one of the keys to the UAHS principal's success—his ability to get parents involved in their children's education. For parents who traditionally have not had opportunities to develop the social capital that would be educationally beneficial to their children, NAAPID provides a venue for parents, school staff, and community members to develop meaningful relationships that lead to educational advantages for their children.

- *Parent breakfasts.* Parent breakfasts occur on four Saturday mornings throughout the school year at UAHS. The purpose is to get parents into the school—meeting with teachers and other school staff—in a situation that is not dominated by conversations about their children's academic or social behaviors. In fact, during the breakfasts UAHS teachers do not broach topics about specific students or academic progress at all. Rather, school staff, students, parents, and community members discuss general issues regarding education, or any other topics, in a manner that is safe and comfortable for all.
- *Report card delivery.* Every student's report card is personally delivered to the student's home. The principal and teachers divide and rotate the responsibility of delivering the report cards. In a television interview, a popular television anchor berates uninvolved parents who don't care about their kids because they don't show up in the school; the UAHS school leader responds, "I don't have any parents that don't show up; I *go* to my parents, and maybe we *should* reach out in the schools." This reaching out to parents allows teachers/leaders to speak directly to parents about their children, providing social capital and thus avenues to academic help for children and their families. In visit after visit, parents developed strong relationships with the principal and teachers, and would often get general advice about their child's welfare. For example, in one particular visit, the principal delivered a report card to the family of a student named Sheila. The family and principal spoke of Shelia

for perhaps only five minutes of the two-hour-long visit. The remainder of the time, the school leader spoke with Sheila's mother, grandmother, and other school-aged relatives (siblings, cousins, and a younger uncle) about educational opportunities and avenues for success. The visits resulted in Shelia's caregivers (mother and grandmother) becoming informed and taking action to improve the educational opportunities for all of their children, including Shelia's siblings.

- *Open school invitation to parents.* The principal at UAHS allows parents to come into the school or their child's class at any time without prior arrangements. Parents interviewed for this study resented not being allowed to come to see their children at the traditional schools in the district; they felt UAHS was more accommodating of their circumstances and liked the openness of the school. Many parents of UAHS students worked second and third shifts at local car manufacturer plants, which did not allow them to visit schools during traditional parent-teacher conference times. Thus, the principal had an open-door policy. One parent who frequently had an evening shift enjoyed his accessibility to the school principal: "I can come see him at any time, it don't matter. At [the other school], I had to wait weeks just to see the principal."

- *Introductory interviews.* The principal interviews every single student and his or her parent(s) or caregivers before allowing the student admission to the school. Though it is a requirement for entry into the school, he has not turned any new student away; operationally, the entrance interviews serve as a way to initiate and inform parents of the structure and mechanisms that regulate the parents' social capital. Therefore, in the interviews, the principal informs parents about the Saturday morning breakfasts, the delivery of report cards and other home visitations, and NAAPID. He seeks a verbal commitment from parents that they will be involved in these social capital–producing mechanisms; all parents so far have agreed, and most overwhelmingly follow through with their commitment.

This list is neither universal nor exhaustive. The question is: What could you actually do in your schools to allow parents to establish social networks and relationships with other families and people in power? How much would it cost a school or district to give teachers three "community" days per year to visit the communities they serve? How far would it go in establishing rapport and trust, and is it worth the money? I argue, yes. A final note is that teachers must be supported in ways that would allow them to establish meaningful relationships with minoritized families.[9] This requires that culturally responsive school leaders devote resources—and as the bulleted list above indicates, not always financial resources—to establishing networks that will equitably facilitate power in schools toward minoritized families.

"I Thought Learning Was What You Cared About Most!": Funds of Knowledge and Cultural Capital of Minoritized Students

> Who wants to go to college? It's fine; you can be who you are. I don't care who you *say* you are. I wanna know who is going to college! [Every student in the room raised their hand expressing their plan to attend college.]
>
> —JOE

Culturally responsive school leaders promote school environments that embrace cultural aspects associated with minoritized student identity. At UAHS, though Joe was over seventy and was not an avid hip-hop fan, he deeply supported his students' identities, including hip-hop-oriented identities. The statement above came from a dialogue between Joe and a group of minoritized students at UAHS. The UAHS principal promoted a school culture that embraced the minoritized student identities, and encouraged academic identities at the same time (i.e., students seeing themselves as high achievers and crafting long-term educational goals). His statements—"I don't care who you *say* you are" and, in another interview, "We accept students as they come; I just want them here, 'cause if they are here, I can help them"—suggest his willingness to embrace student identities that were largely marginalized in Davistown's traditional schools.

At UAHS, Joe demanded that teachers keep students in their classes and actually learn to "teach the students' cultures in your classes." In a district that has always had a very severe discipline gap, this was not insignificant. But more importantly, when teachers learned that they would not be allowed to exclude minoritized identities as "aggressive" or "insubordinate," for example, it began a process that pushed teachers to recognize and engage the cultural capital of their students. In a focus group interview, a student we'll call "TJ" was always leaving his seat without permission, and explained that he was not accustomed to sitting in a chair for long periods of time: "From where I'm from, I didn't just used to sit there. My dad, my uncles, and all of us are movement-oriented people, so yeah, I might get up to sharpen a pencil or just to take a stroll in the class. But that was no reason to put me out, and Joe didn't let it happen."

TJ's self-description of leaving his seat without permission and the frequently berated behavior of "speaking too loud" or "speaking out of turn" are all behaviors that led to frequent suspensions in Davistown's traditional public schools. In four years at UAHS, TJ received neither referrals nor suspensions, and as a result felt a sense of belonging. Grace, another UAHS student who had been repeatedly suspended in the traditional schools, added that "African Americans are a loud people; we yell at church, we yell at home, and if you come into our house and it's quiet, something is wrong."

Thus, changes came about not so much because Joe went around enlightening teachers about specific student identities or cultural behaviors. Rather, it was a matter of not accommodating teachers who were dismissive of *any* minoritized student identities. With the principal's direction, teachers at UAHS accepted culturally nuanced expressions of language and music and, most important, behaviors that were not in violation of school rules but may have been uncomfortable for teachers. So, what is perhaps the biggest indication of the acceptance of minoritized cultural capital was, in fact, that students were *not* shamed, teased, mocked, or penalized for cultural behaviors. Particular types of dress, language, resistance to authority or insubordination, and aggressive posturing and play are examples of cultural student behaviors that were punished in the district's traditional schools, but were humanized at UAHS. In other words, cultural experiences of traditional White middle-class students received no preferential treatment. The following are structural (i.e., administrative) elements that are essential in promoting culturally responsive school environments that embrace minoritized student identities:

- *Resisting exclusionary practices.* Culturally responsive school leaders identify, protect, and honor minoritized student identities. They understand the community-based contexts from which the identities come, and they humanize these identities in school. They deem it unacceptable for their staff to criticize, shame, emotionally abuse, dismiss, or ignore student identities. If a staff member enacts any exclusionary practices toward these identities, culturally responsive principals put a stop to them.
- *Redirecting teachers toward student learning.* Culturally responsive school leaders redirect teacher's exclusionary practices and understandings by pushing teachers to lose their fears of different student behaviors. Unfortunately, teachers often focus on student identities that they find distasteful, and pressure students to change to identities that are more familiar. Instead, the leader(s) encourages (or pushes) teachers to focus on helping

the students to develop an academic identity and achieve academic success.

- *Redirecting teachers into learning student identity and cultural capital.* Culturally responsive school leaders develop teachers into being culturally responsive, and to having more positive and accurate understandings of students and communities. This means that teachers must learn to recognize their students' cultural capital and to honor that capital, rather than to imagine deficit-oriented stereotypes of their students. Leaders must facilitate opportunities for teachers to learn about students' cultural capital.

- *Using school resources to build funds of knowledge.* The culturally responsive school leaders provide opportunities for students and families to share their life experiences in safe, nonexploitative, and nonexoticizing ways. These community-based life experiences are not merely shared, but are recorded and used to inform pedagogy, curriculum, and policy in schools. This must be ongoing, and will enlighten teachers on the ever-changing, dynamic student identities that they serve. This work might look different in different spaces; for example, in Indigenous spaces, it could be staff participation in storytelling; but in Latinx spaces, it might be teachers volunteering and participating in community-based panels (or interactive forums) about bolstering safe "sanctuary" spaces in and around the school district.

- *Mentoring and modeling inclusiveness and identity confluence.* Last, culturally responsive school leaders provide mentoring and modeling of culturally responsive practice in schools. This happens in daily interactions with students and parents, in how students are described in staff meetings and in school documents, in how students are referred to programs, and in who is punished or humanized in school. Since building leaders greatly contribute to school climate and culture, they can set the tone for how these identities are received. Culturally responsive school leaders can be *the* most influential persons in a school in terms of developing an academic identity in students.

All of this indicates that it is not only acceptable and humanizing for minoritized children to keep their identities, but that by doing so, students may actually be more likely to stay in school and even excel.[10] The school principal actively resisted teachers' tendency to exclude at-risk students from school. Though in traditional schools, marginalized students were often suspended, at UAHS space was created so that students could both maintain their own cultural identity and adopt the role of being "smart." They were not criminalized or contained for being Indigenous or Black. The activities in figure 4.1 are designed to help educators move closer to humanizing all student identities.

FIGURE 4.1 Activity (45 days): Humanizing identity in school

In this activity, your team will analyze two sources of programmatic data: the *disciplinary program* and the *special education program*. With a team composed of administrators, educators, teachers, and preferably including community members, look at referrals to these programs from an equity standpoint. In your analysis, answer the following questions about at least 10 percent of the randomly selected referrals:

- What are the top three demographic student groups that are referred to discipline and special education programs?
- Read through the referrals and characterize the language used to describe the students. Select some examples. What are the top five reasons these students were referred to either program?
- Interview twenty students (ten for each program) about how they felt during the referral process, how their parents felt, if they believed they should have been referred, and whether the program helped them (assuming that the process moved beyond the referral).
- Work with the team to identify which of the student behaviors that led to the referral are cultural, and which are not.
- Present the research to staff and school leaders and send a summary of the results to community stakeholders (ensuring accessibility).

continues

FIGURE 4.1 *Continued*

Principal's Task

Form a team to reform the school policy on disciplinary and special education referrals and placement. Ask teachers, leaders, students, and community
members to join the committee. Identify the most vulnerable, most marginalized, and least present families in the district, and establish a work relationship with them. Try to include parents who have had children in the school
who were suspended (especially if multiple times), who were frequently ab-
sent from school, and who are not performing well academically. Ask the entire team to help reform the policies. Do not train the parents and students to
think like you; rather, ask them what they think the policies should look like
based on their life experiences, and based on serving the most marginalized.

Superintendent's Task

Ask each of your principals to conduct similar processes in their schools;
after each school has completed this process, bring all of the plans together
and seek similarities across schools. Craft a district policy based on the
school policies.

CONCLUSION

Students come here and say, "Wow, you know, I feel comfortable here. I don't feel like an outsider; I feel like my thoughts and
my home life is valued, the way I do my hair or dress is valued;
it's not odd, it's not different." We relate to the kids, relate to the
community; we're always trying to figure out how to do that better. We're trying to figure out how to meet their needs; to take
them from where they are to where they need to be, and it's the
best way that we know how.

These words issued by Joe indicate an embrace of minoritized student identities. Before coming to UAHS and encountering a culturally responsive school leader, the school staff neither recognized nor
accepted the cultural and social capital of minoritized students and
their families. Thus, they did not humanize these identities. Minoritized students in the district, particularly Black students, were suspended at a much higher rate than their White classmates, even for

the same offenses. Data that emerged from parent and student interviews suggest that fear or misinterpretation of student posture was quite common in traditional schools. However, this research shows that the devaluation of Black and poor students' social and cultural capital that existed in the district's traditional schools was successfully mitigated by the leadership at UAHS. The school leader would not allow teachers to devalue the students' culture, nor dehumanize student identity. If a teacher sent a child out of his or her classroom for acting aggressive, being "disorderly," or for having hyperghettoized clothing or speech, the principal would send the student back to the classroom so that the teacher could learn how to understand, value, and equitably engage—humanize—that student. The school leader would explain why he did not feel the student should be removed from class, and would mediate and advocate for the student.

My purpose in this chapter has not been to present a simplistic binary of a *tolerant principal* who accepted Indigenous and minoritized identities versus *racist exclusionary principals* in the district's traditional schools. Indeed, the context is far more complex than this, and the fact that Joe often encouraged some behavior modification in his students is suggestive of this complexity. Rather, my point here has been to show how a principal promoted a culture that embraces traditionally minoritized students, and conveyed that they had a place in school and would not be counseled or pushed away because of how they identified or behaved. Fighting or inflicting other types of physical harm was the only reason that a student would be isolated until the causes could be addressed. In addition to his own advocacy and leadership behaviors, Joe taught and encouraged these children and their parents to advocate for their own school inclusion. So if a teacher chastised students for their dress, or for "aggressive behavior," the students and their families learned to resist and to press for their place in school. Table 4.2 can help educators recognize and honor community-based assets of minoritized students.

TABLE 4.2 Inclusive capital and funds of knowledge

Issue in school	Cultural capital/funds of knowledge questions	Social capital questions
Student disengages academically.	• Has the principal created opportunities for teachers to do community-based research, which would allow them to present cultural knowledge in class?	• Has the principal established relationships with community members, which would allow educators access to community-based knowledge, experiences, and epistemology? • Has the school initiated a learning network that would lead to high academic achievement among minoritized students, such as academic mentoring and tutoring in the classroom?
Student chooses to leave school before graduation.	• Do school leaders and teachers fully understand how schooling is viewed by students and why it is (or is not) important to their communities?	• Has the principal connected students with people with similar experiences, colleges or technical programs, or other community resources, and held critical conversations about school completion?
Student chooses not to follow teachers' directives.	• Has the school explored community-based ways of engaging with student agency and protest?	• Has the principal established community mentoring programs that help students understand outcomes connected to their decisions?
Parent chooses not to respond to teacher phone calls or invitations to school.	• Do school leaders and educators understand community-based perceptions of their school, and the history of how this school has engaged the community?	• Do school leaders have alternative networks that would allow educators to share space (and interests) with parents, even if it is a nonschool space? Have leaders helped teachers be comfortable in that space?
Teacher sends minoritized students out of the classroom with disciplinary referrals.	• Does the school leader have a learning program in place that would allow teachers to understand and value minoritized students' funds of knowledge? Are offending teachers mentored?	• Can the school leader place teachers with both a teacher mentor and a community mentor who could help make the classroom management culturally responsive?

TABLE 4.2 *Continued*

Issue in school	Cultural capital/funds of knowledge questions	Social capital questions
Teacher does not have a culturally responsive curriculum and refuses to include content relevant for minoritized students.	• Does the school leader have a learning program in place that would allow teachers to access community-based knowledge?	• Can the school leader place teachers with both a teacher mentor and a community mentor who can help them make pedagogical practices culturally responsive?
Principal does not understand (or prioritize) cultural responsiveness, but many of the teachers do.	• Can teachers (or other building administrators) use official school data, or student and parent voice, to present a case to the principal?	• Can other teachers (or other leaders) in the building partner with parents, students, community members/organizations, or district-level administrators to make this issue a priority?
Principal does not challenge the actions of exclusionary teachers, and confirms their actions with administrative power.	• Can other teachers (or other leaders) in the building use equity data, or equity audits, to encourage the principal to challenge and resist institutionalization of exclusionary practice?	• Can other teachers (or other leaders) in the building partner with parents, students, community members/organizations, or district-level administrators to challenge exclusionary practices?

Indeed, there has been much research in recent years that pushes teachers to reject viewing students, communities, and community-based Indigenous knowledge in a negative way. Rather, this knowledge should be viewed not only as an asset, but also as crucial parts of pedagogy and curriculum within classrooms. Again, Gonzalez, Moll, and Amanti describe this concept in their seminal work:

People are competent, they have knowledge, and their life experiences have given them that knowledge. Our claim is that firsthand research experiences with families allow one to document this competence and knowledge. It is this engagement that opened up many possibilities for positive pedagogical actions. The theoretical concepts presented in this book, a funds of knowledge approach, facilitates a systematic and powerful way to represent communities in terms of resources, the wherewithal they possess, and how to harness these resources for classroom teaching.[11]

This can be liberating for educators because it allows them to think of their students in the best possible light. Teachers can go into communities to learn of the Indigenous and minoritized student identities; they will look to their communities as places where they can learn to be better teachers; they will learn from community-based epistemologies to enrich their own curriculums; they will resist attempts to "change" students and replace Indigenous identities with "academic" identities; and they will resist exclusionary practices toward students from minoritized communities. But what does this research mean for school leaders? To answer this question, we must consider school-level systemic practices, cultures, and climates. We must also consider issues around student identity; in this chapter, I do not go into great detail on specific student identities, but rather consider how *all* student identities can be honored and humanized in school. I argue that CRSL is concerned with the following questions as it pertains to embracing minoritized student identities:

- What are the ways that minoritized student identities are excluded in school, and how do CRSL principals recognize them?
- How do CRSL principals promote welcoming school environments that embrace Indigenous and minoritized student identities as positive and normal?
- What must CRSL principals do to ensure that educators (and other school staff) celebrate, humanize, and support all student identities, and connect these minoritized identities with classroom pedagogy?

IDENTITY CONFLUENCE. In this chapter, I argue for an *identity confluence* of minoritized student identities. Traditional approaches of shaming or disparaging Indigenous and minoritized student identities are futile (because students will not change) and oppressive (because they promote a deficit view of these students). I strongly criticize efforts to push students into new identities based on deficit understandings of Indigenous and minoritized students. If a student portrays herself or himself as a type of gangster, a hip-hop personality, or even an athlete—all student identities that were disparaged or rejected by some teachers in this study—the identities should be embraced. In fact, I argue that no Indigenous or community-based identity should prevent teachers from teaching (and humanizing) minoritized students. School leaders, though, are responsible for promoting a school context that embraces *all* minoritized student identities, and they must push back against teachers who demonstrate an intolerance of any students. At UAHS, Joe did not disparage student identities, nor did he allow his teachers to do so. Rather, he pushed himself and his teachers to construct a school environment that would encourage academic behaviors along *with* all other student identities.[12] CRSL behaviors that support and humanize *identity confluence* have several integral components:

1. *Understanding your own history and epistemological bias.* This is a necessary first step because otherwise you will not be able to understand how you are oppressing minoritized identities, especially if they are different from yours.

2. *Centering children above yourself; preventing your fears, feelings, disagreements, and emotions (etc.) from arresting this work.* This has been one of the major inhibitors to doing culturally responsive work; leaders and staff almost instinctively first tend to their own feelings, and thus end up marginalizing the treatment of minoritized students.

3. *Distinguishing between identity and behaviors.* Embrace all student identities, but recognize that some behaviors (such as

smoking) are harmful for students. Gain wide community and student support on what those behaviors are in order to discourage them. Behaviors linked to identity—such as dress, language, mannerisms, interactions with others—should not be penalized (via policy or shaming).

4. *Humanizing minoritized identities.* Understand that to accept some identities (e.g., White, middle-class, docile, etc.) while rejecting others (Black, gangster, street, etc.) is bigotry and is an act of violence. Minoritized student identities must be treated with the same respect, honor, belongingness, and inclusiveness as all other identities, within all school activities.

5. *Learning the "funds of knowledge" from minoritized identities.* As school leaders shift from being schoolcentric to being community-centric, and as they center minoritized student identities in the school, they must be intentional about how this happens. Community members and students should be the only source for this recentering. Schools have to find ways to learn Indigenous and ancestral knowledge, and then (a) offer distinct cultural studies courses and (b) weave this Indigenous/ancestral knowledge throughout all aspects of schooling, including policy making.

HUMANIZING STUDENTS. Humanizing students is connected to *identity confluence* in that they both accept the Indigenous identity of students, but identity confluence is concerned with adding positive academic behaviors to the ways that students already view themselves, or self-identify. Dehumanization of minoritized students is connected to historical oppression that predates the establishment of US schools. In other words, it is deeply connected to histories of settler colonialism, and the exploitation of Indigenous peoples and lands. The works of scholars like Grosfoguel and Mielants and Mignolo suggest that European colonization models have contributed to the types of dehumanization we experience in US schools today.[13] This involves seeing minoritized people and communities as less than human or savages, and therefore made to be subjects of Europeans who would help the minoritized people by colonizing them. As colonizing empires—in particular the Spanish, English, French, Dutch, Belgian, and later the United States—realized that they needed the land and bodies of non-Whites in the accumulation of wealth, they took those lands and bodies by brute force. Colonizers invented narratives about Indigenous people as a way to justify their exploitative actions. In other words, Europeans vanquished African, Native American, Asian, and Arab people and lands not because they were greedy and needed natural resources, bodies, and lands (in their rationalizations) but because they were "helping" the natives out of their savagery, barbarism, and paganism. Such *dehumanizing* narratives, however, would follow minoritized communities into the modern era and into public schools today. By humanizing and honoring minoritized identities, educators and school leaders resist the impulse to colonize the identities of minoritized students.

HUMANIZING HIP-HOP AT UAHS. This chapter highlights CRSL behaviors that humanize minoritized student identities. At UAHS, specific school structures were in place that contributed to this student humanization. Though Joe was several generations removed from the young students he served, he built spaces into the school day for discourse around student identity. This was most pronounced around students identifying with behaviors, dress, speaking styles, and performances imbued in hip-hop music and culture. To further clarify this, I have included research on what scholars refer to as *cultural capital* and the ways that knowledge can enrich school contexts (for more on this, see Yosso's work on *community cultural wealth*).[14] At UAHS, behaviors such as sagging pants, marijuana use, and profanity, as well as behaviors deemed to be "aggressive," "disrespectful," or "insubordinate," were all viewed with the cultural responsiveness that they deserved, and were subordinate to the students' personal and academic needs. The results were truly remarkable, and contributed to the academic success of UAHS students (grades and graduation rate). But why? I contend that when students are allowed to be themselves, and are not overpoliced and pressured to change, they can then get on with the business of learning. Minoritized students can clearly see bigotry (e.g., asking only them to change while not challenging the White, middle-class identities in school), and they can then choose to resist educators. But the opposite can also happen, and did happen at UAHS. When educators were willing to say what teacher Michael told Marwan—"I ain't gonna trip on your gangster swag, and I will accept you as you are, and I will just focus on learning"—Marwan was also willing to learn and take school seriously. But most UAHS educators even went further than what teacher Michael expressed here. They not only allowed these identities to exist, but they also humanized and celebrated all UAHS student identities. They found the worth in the identities, and they learned from them. The traditional barriers between school and communities were erased, and UAHS students found ways to incorporate their new academic identities into their lives.

CHAPTER 4

Discussion Questions

For Principals

1. List the five most prevalent identities among minoritized students in your school and discover the following about each group:
   - What are the primary elements of how the students self-identify?
   - How have these student identities been historically received in your school?

- What strengths can these identities offer in shaping school culture, policy, and curriculum?
- How are these identities influenced by and positioned in their communities?
- How comfortable are my teachers (and other staff) with these identities? How are these identities currently minoritized in school? By whom?
- How am I regularly measuring the treatment of these minoritized students?

2. What is our funds of knowledge learning program, so that teachers can (a) regularly learn about life experiences and educational priorities of minoritized students and families and (b) improve the school culture, climate, and policies in humanizing ways?

For Teacher Leaders and Equity Leadership Team

1. What are strategies we can use to engage teachers who are resistant to this work?
2. What are the culturally responsive mentoring networks needed for teacher mentors, and for mentors from the community?

For Superintendents and District Office Staff

1. How will the district use current data to measure the humanization and acceptance of minoritized students and families?
2. How will educators incorporate funds of knowledge learning, equity audits, and other nontraditional data to understand community-based voices, and then use this data to impact district-level policy?

HUMANIZING SCHOOL COMMUNITIES OF PRACTICE

Culturally Responsive Leaders in the Shaping of Curriculum and Instruction

I'm not going to let the teachers have their way with the kids.

—JOE, UAHS principal

The chapters thus far have examined ways that school leaders can involve the community to make schooling more inclusive and humanizing for minoritized students and communities. This chapter looks at how leaders foster culturally responsive teachers, curricula, and instruction. Is it enough for school leaders to be *instructional* leaders and *transformational* leaders? Should CRSL be thought of as distinct from these types of leadership—something to engage in once a year—or is it more appropriate to think of CRSL as infused throughout all other types of leadership? Can principals focus solely on raising test scores, and if they do, is this marginalizing or dehumanizing toward students? What are the *leadership behaviors* that foster culturally responsive curricula and teaching practices?

Most traditional leaders believe that their jobs are to improve student performance by providing instructional leadership, usually measured by test scores, grades, and graduation rates. Many educators (and even researchers) compartmentalize "community" as outreach that must be done in addition to these more traditional components of schooling. But throughout this book, I contest this notion.

I wonder: First, what do communities want for their own children, and second, in what ways do the experiences and knowledge of parents and community members improve learning for students? How can principals leverage community epistemology and voice to improve how teachers teach? I have discussed notions of neighborhood community in the preceding four chapters. In this chapter, however, I address the *school community*, and how knowledge and epistemologies from the broader neighborhood communities can influence, shape, and ultimately reform leadership and structures in schools. I diagram this connection in figure 5.1, where I compare traditional and culturally responsive school leadership structures. The figure suggests that centering the role of parents and communities is crucial in the development of curricula and content, and is needed to create a humanizing learning environment for students.

FIGURE 5.1 Influences on student performance

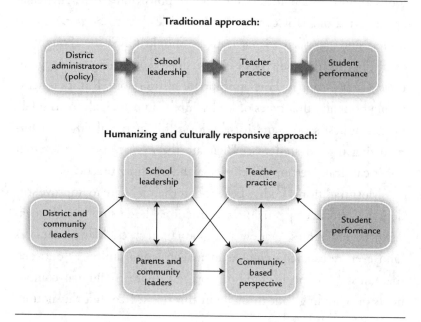

Although one of the key roles of culturally responsive school leaders is to help teachers develop humanizing and culturally responsive behaviors, it is one of the least studied aspects of CRSL. I suggest this is true for several reasons. For one, school leadership has been rigidly and traditionally defined. In other words, despite expanded leadership traditions in recent years, it has been hard to separate school leadership from the traditional "manager" role of a hierarchical employee who "puts out our fires" and implements policies handed down from the district or state. Second, the scholarship on CRSL has generously discussed how leaders should be critical, intellectual, and community based, but it has been limited in addressing how leaders should engage some of the more traditional components of leadership, such as how one can be a "culturally responsive instructional leader." A final shortfall of the literature has been for CRSL scholarship to almost completely rely on culturally relevant pedagogy/teaching literature to explain aspects of leadership. While this literature is indeed valuable, I believe that leaders have a unique mandate and set of responsibilities. In this chapter, I use this scholarship to understand how Joe used community and community-based student behaviors as a driving force for instructional leadership and curricula development in his school.

Research also has recognized that certain school features can have an impact on teacher learning and performance.[1] For example, scholars find that school features such as professional learning communities, the trust and respect that teachers have for each other, teachers' sense of their own responsibility for student learning, the extent to which students are supported, and school culture and climate are all related to student achievement. This all suggests that these school features are crucial components of developing a *culturally responsive school culture*.

Throughout this chapter, I share evidence about how Joe developed culturally responsive teachers at UAHS through his influence on school culture and climate. I include examples of how Joe encouraged teachers to "use the students' life stories in the lessons 'cause it's got to be relevant," as he explained to one of his science teachers. Like most teachers, those at UAHS largely reported that they had not been trained as culturally responsive educators in their college teacher-training programs. Joe practiced informal teacher development by *modeling* and *mentoring* his teachers toward cultural responsiveness. If teachers resisted and did not bring student experiences and community-based understandings into their classrooms, he more assertively pushed them toward community engagement connected to their craft. Though school leaders themselves do not necessarily lead instruction in classrooms, this work suggests they can nonetheless yield considerable pedagogical and curricular influence in schools. But how is instructional leadership connected to community? The following exchange between Joe and Mary, a UAHS math teacher, gives some clues:

JOE: I wanted to talk to you about Tamaria, because I heard from her aunt today.

MARY: Yeah, I talked to her too.

JOE: Well, she has concerns that her niece is failing math, and she can't graduate without it.

MARY: I've talked to her. I've talked to her. I've talked to her. She's not changing. She's not completing her assignments. And I've spoken to her aunt. I don't think she has an interest in math, and that's fine, but I don't know what else I can do.

JOE: We know who the kids are when we get them, and I recognize the challenges. But that's not an excuse. We can't blame them, 'cause it's not gonna solve the problem; we have to blame ourselves.

MARY: I'm all ears if you have some suggestions for me. I am
literally at wit's end. I don't know what to do.

JOE: Utilize the community. Utilize the community.

This exchange emphasized two points: (1) the need for teachers and school leaders to take collective responsibility for student
performance; and (2) using community-based knowledge can help
teachers achieve this goal. Joe's insistence that Mary "utilize the community" meant that she should literally connect with people within
the community, such as Tamaria's aunt, as well as with various sources
of "knowledge" in the community. As Nieto and Gay suggest, learning should be built on prior knowledge.[2] Within the two months following this conversation with Joe, Mary had invited two community
members into her room to speak to her students about how they use
math in their lives. One of the speakers was a local hip-hop music
producer who spoke about the many ways that he uses math in book-
ing shows, measuring music tracks, paying artists, funding tours, buy-
ing equipment, and generally staying profitable. In this case, Mary
was not using cultural knowledge to teach aspects of geometry to
ninth- and tenth-grade students; rather, she invited the speaker with
the intention of making math relevant to students who were interested in hip-hop—something with which UAHS students identified.

The second guest was a local barber, and his class involvement
was relevant for a geometry lesson on angles. In this case, the barber used angles to teach students how to "fade" or "timmy" hair of
Black students. The barber demonstrated how, by using various angles, he was able to blend the lines away in one student's hair. Mary
then had students use those angles throughout the geometry lesson, such as when they discussed different types of triangles. This
use of community-based knowledge in her lessons seemed to lead
students—including Tamaria—to become highly engrossed in the

lesson. This example indicates how Joe pushed teachers not only to share collective responsibility, but also to take individual responsibility for how their students were doing in their classes.

HUMANIZING COMMUNITIES OF PRACTICE

While I affirm that knowledge from the neighborhood community is crucial, I argue that this knowledge must be translated and infused into professional, school-based communities of practice. So I ask: Can *professional learning communities* (PLCs) be culturally responsive? School communities in which all people are bonded by a vision to help children—and then actually commit to learning together— are necessary for school improvement. While much has been written about PLCs within schools, few have described how they can be equitable, humanizing, and culturally responsive.[3] Indeed, I have visited many schools that have PLCs, but also have egregious disciplinary and achievement gaps. In the many schools I have visited over the years, I rarely witnessed a PLC that had incorporated cultural responsiveness throughout its activities. I agree with Stoll and Seashore Louis that teachers must engage in "sharing and critically interrogating their practice in an ongoing, reflective, collaborative, inclusive, learning-oriented, growth-promoting way."[4] But I use this chapter to show that school leaders should place equity and cultural responsiveness at the center of student learning; that is, PLCs must be culturally responsive.

But how can this be accomplished? School leaders must work with parents and teachers to embrace equity in addition to academic excellence. At UAHS, Joe would consistently praise the work of teachers, but would always ask, "How does that help *our* kids?" The way he emphasized *our* meant something to him and his staff; he was consistently questioning: How can minoritized kids (even outside of school) and their parents benefit from this work?

Stoll and Seashore Louis describe four components of PLCs: (1) professional learning; (2) learning within the context of a cohesive group; (3) a focus on collective knowledge; and (4) activity that occurs within an ethic of interpersonal caring that permeates the lives of teachers, students, and school leaders.[5] I would add to this description of PLCs an emphasis on community. This goes beyond focusing on the ways that PLCs can include parents to how they can involve all *community-based people* (parents and grandparents, barbers and other local businesspeople, community leaders, older siblings, UAHS alumni, local personalities, etc.) and *community-based knowledge* (ways of viewing the world, the meaning of knowledge and how its transmitted, acceptable behavior, etc.). Here are leadership tips to making the core components of PLCs more culturally responsive:

1. Connect All PLC Learnings to Cultural Responsiveness

All PLC driving questions should include language that centers cultural responsiveness. In addition, culturally responsive follow-up questions should respond to students and their communities. For example, in table 5.1 I present one way to make the four driving questions of PLCs more culturally responsive by adding subquestions.[6]

2. Include Collective and Individual Responsibility in PLC Discussions

In prior studies, researchers placed heavy emphasis on the collective responsibility of teachers. That is, as a staff teachers must collectively accept responsibility for the treatment, and ultimately the successes and failures, of children in school. But the research here extends this in two crucial ways. First, for teachers to acquire equitable and humanizing behaviors, school leaders must address the practices of individual teachers. In other words, school leaders should discuss whether or not individual teachers have culturally responsive instruction and content, and whether or not this bears out in equitable achievement for minoritized students. Individual teacher evaluations

TABLE 5.1 How to make PLCs more culturally responsive

Common driving questions of PLCs	Sample subquestions
What do we want all students to learn?	• Does what we want students to learn include minoritized communities' knowledge? Have we asked the community what students should learn? • Does the knowledge connect to the communities and experiences of minoritized students? • Is what we want students to learn (i.e., knowledge) *beneficial* to minoritized communities?
How will we know if and when they have learned it?	• Are the scales and rubrics used culturally responsive? Are the questions culturally biased? • What are nontraditional ways of measuring the knowledge of minoritized students? • How will the community perspectives be included in how learning is measured? • What are the best ways for *our* students to show what they know?
How will we teach it?	• Are the instructional methods culturally responsive and inclusive? • How are parents and community members used to help connect instruction to student communities/lives?
How will we respond if some students do not learn? How will we respond if the students have already learned?	• How will we use critical self-reflection techniques to understand when (and why) some minoritized students are not responding to our instruction and content? • How will we take responsibility (individually and collectively) if minoritized students are not learning?

and discussions already happen in specific content areas. However, school leaders are much less engaged in discussions around race and cultural responsiveness, in large part because of administrator discomfort with discussing histories of White and Western oppression of minoritized peoples. Palmer notes that teachers "are scared to be considered racist when they say the wrong thing. Principals have to start from a place of conscious vulnerability—not easy!"[7]

Second, PLC discussions of individual and collective responsibility must not only extend to student performance; they must also include notions of community. In this regard, culturally responsive school leaders should be concerned with how teachers, both as individuals and as a collective, are engaging community.

- How can community-based knowledge be used to improve teaching and curricula for minoritized children? (For example, as discussed in chapters 3 and 4, how can the knowledge and lessons within rap music or Indigenous storytelling be centered as the content used in science, social studies, or language classes?)
- How do community members (parents, students, community leaders, community-based organizations, etc.) contribute to discussions about whether or not the collective staffs and individual teachers are culturally responsive?
- What are culturally responsive ways that community members can become part of the collective? (*Note:* The purpose of community partnership is ineffective if schools continue to "train" parents in how to be involved and contribute. Rather, schools should avoid this type of colonization, and seek to have authentic, community-based collaborations despite educator discomfort and the perceived inexperience of community members.)

3. Include Community-Based People and Perspectives in PLC Discussions

Throughout this book, I have emphasized a number of practices—some to include and others to avoid—as school leaders approach community. I have shared several approaches from UAHS, but every community will have culturally unique histories and nuances that leaders should consider as they find their own way to lead with the community. Here is a recap of some of the more prominent don'ts and dos:

DON'T:
- Colonize parents by "training" them to accept schoolcentric views. I am familiar with the Chicago Local School Councils studies, and the claims that parents are not properly equipped to lead. But are all current leaders? Are similar claims leveled at White, middle-class parents? This research suggests that authentic parent/community perspectives only enrich schooling and learning.
- Suppress community-based perspectives by limiting them to meetings organized by schools; rather, leave channels of communication with the community open.
- Limit community engagement to school spaces or conferences.
- Rely on the voices of parents and community residents who are already the most engaged with the schools; rather, seek out voices that are often *not* heard.
- Make assumptions about minoritized people or communities based on your own unique experiences and histories.

DO:
- Include both community members and community-based knowledge in how schools are organized, managed, reformed, and evaluated.
- Put structures in place so that educators can go into communities and learn from community residents.
- Use community-based knowledge and people to resist racism and other forms of oppression (for example, how can you include the ways the refugee communities have resisted oppression and racism in their communities?).

- Use community-based knowledge and people to build curricula and teaching methods, and to learn culturally responsive ways of responding to student behavior.
- Use the voice of Indigenous elders and parents (and others carrying ancestral knowledge) to contribute to all aspects of schooling.

4. Use Data (Equity Audits) to Center Equity in Decision Making

Educators and leaders pride themselves on being data-driven. Schools have a culture of disseminating data; they report standardized test scores and discuss them in meetings throughout the year. Reforms are often based on this data. Data about community demographics, student enrollment, and performance all contribute to annual plans. Unfortunately, some teachers even divulge data on student performance in front of the class, believing that reporting out poor results will embarrass the student enough to complete assignments. But many of these same educators and leaders do not want this data-driven culture expanded to include their own progress around issues of equity and cultural responsiveness. In a recent equity audit that I performed, here are a few comments that were issued by educators and leaders in that district:

> Why should I complete the survey for the equity audit? Just so they can tell us how racist we are?
>
> —EDUCATOR who refused to partake in the equity audit

> It has to be anonymous, or else no one will complete it.
>
> —DISTRICT LEADER who requested the equity audit

> In the student focus group at one school, they [administrators] put all "A" students in the focus group interviews. The principal didn't put any of the students in the interview group who might have said that they experienced racism.
>
> —EQUITY TEAM LEADER familiar with student demographics

All three of these statements indicate a tension these educators had around issues of equity—I noticed hesitation, reluctance, resistance, fear, and even defensiveness from many individuals I encountered despite the district's being nearly 50 percent students of color. Unfortunately, I have found similar sentiments in nearly all of the districts in which I have performed equity audits.[8] Even though educators are willing to discuss *academic* data, they are often unwilling to discuss or uncomfortable when discussing data that might indicate they are racist or oppressive. Yet CRSL requires direct, constant discussion of equity data, which can be used to:

- Frame the agendas around "achievement gaps" and "discipline gaps"
- Identify how resources should be structured to address inequities
- Identify educators who need extra support in serving minoritized students
- Measure how minoritized students/families are experiencing school climate
- Determine whether some communities are privileged or marginalized by the school
- Monitor equity in programs/classes such as advanced placement (AP), STEM, disciplinary, ESL, special education, clubs, student government, and so on
- Craft all future equity reforms with accurate, aligned, and comprehensive equity data

In essence, a comprehensive equity audit must be the starting point for CRSL and equity reforms. As a researcher, former leader, and equity audit specialist, I developed my equity audits to look at four basic areas:

1. *Equity trends.* Equity audits must examine data across multiple levels (including student, teacher, grade, program, school, and district levels) to highlight patterns of and differences in student equity.

2. *Survey data.* Equity audits must collect data measures on core equity areas. Based on the scholarly research, we find nine core equity areas that contribute to equity or inequities in schools, including school culture and climate, community engagement, and culturally responsive teaching, among other areas.

3. *Policy analysis.* Equity audits must conduct a critical analysis of school policies that may disproportionately affect minoritized students.

4. *CRSL.* Equity audits must test for culturally responsive curriculum, pedagogy, and leadership practices, among other core equity areas.

5. Teacher Evaluation

It is well established in the literature that promoting culturally responsive instruction is a crucial role of culturally responsive school leaders.[9] At UAHS, this meant Joe constantly pulled student perspectives into how teachers thought about their instruction. In one instance, he kept asking one of the older white male science teachers, Blake: "How do you draw kids in who don't look and talk like you?" When Blake responded, "I just bring good science content and experimentation," Joe pressed further, and insisted that if he (Blake) does not have a strong relationship with the children, good content is not enough. Joe explained, "It was once said that a good lesson plan is good classroom management. Not true with Blacks. They've got to trust you and know that you care for them, or nothing else matters!"

As a researcher who prepares countless school leaders, I have taken many exchanges like this to heart. I have come to believe that if our teacher evaluation tools are not explicit about equity and cultural responsiveness, schooling will continue to underserve minoritized students. Figure 5.2 represents my thoughts on how I would adapt Charlotte Danielson's framework of teacher evaluations, but with an explicit focus on culturally responsive leadership practice.[10] This is less a critique of prior teacher evaluation frameworks like Danielson's, and more a recognition that most frameworks have never really addressed issues of equity and social justice. Consequently, even schools that use such frameworks often still have deep and persistent inequities in education.

CENTERING COMMUNITY IN SCHOOLCENTRIC REFORMS

State standards are not what drive what we do.
What matters to me is what's best for the kids; show me
how something supports the kids, and I'll support it.

—JOE

Culturally responsive school leaders prioritize community interests above all else and seek ways to align the community with educational reforms and policy. Joe's comment above pushed back against traditional forms of school leadership. The context of this statement was that he was challenging a staff meeting conversation about student welfare, which was being dominated by test scores. Three UAHS teachers were focusing on their students' Michigan Educational Assessment Program (MEAP) scores. One teacher, Lisa, offered: "Joe, everybody is talking about how great we are, but if we don't get these test scores up, we are not going to be an effective school." Becky, the union representative, agreed: "Yep, state aid is dependent on it. I mean, the reading scores are up, but we've been struggling to get math up for years!" Joe pushed back: "I thought we were talking about how to serve the community and what's best for kids?" Aaron, a first-year teacher, responded, "Well, I thought that when MEAP

FIGURE 5.2 Framework for teacher evaluations with a focus on culturally responsive leadership

Domain 1: Planning and Preparation

CRSL items:

- Design instruction and assessments that use community epistemology and knowledge
- Set individualized instructional outcomes

Demonstrate knowledge of:

- How student experiences are connected to content and pedagogy
- Oppressive historical barriers for minoritized students
- Unique learning styles of all students in classroom
- Community-based expectations for schooling and learning
- Understanding which student groups need more of what resources

Domain 2: The Classroom Environment

CRSL items:

- Organize class space that reflects how learning happens in community spaces
- Establish expectations informed by representative community folks and parents
- Establish an environment in which minoritized students understand middle class White expectations
- Establish classroom rules, procedures, and consequences that
  - promote a culture of excellence and equity
  - connect with students on a personal level
  - create an environment of humanization and anti-oppression

Domain 3: Instruction

CRSL items:

- Communicate equitably with students
- Show concern for and willingness to confront challenges faced by students
- Use community epistemology/experience in lessons
- Convey content in ways that mirror student/community histories
- Understand feedback from students' perception of your teaching

Domain 4: Professional Responsibilities

CRSL items:

- Critically self-reflect on role of culturally responsive teaching and anti-oppression
- Advocate for community-based goals
- Participate in a humanizing professional community
- Show willingness to confront/challenge colleagues who dehumanize minoritized students

scores improve, that we were serving the community." However, Joe disagreed, asking, "How does improving scores improve the community? How does that happen? Jobs? Less crime? More opportunity? 'Cause I haven't seen that. And that is what I'm talking about right now: the community."

Many school leaders feel compelled to encourage teachers to "teach to the test." The pressure has been so intense that a culture of testing has led to a culture of cheating (on standardized tests) in some districts. It has been difficult to show how neighborhoods, parents, or communities actually benefit from increased test scores and other educational reforms. Joe was challenging his teachers to imagine how there might be alignment between school and community, and at the very least, how academic conversations should not be dominated by issues with no direct connection to community empowerment and improvement.

Standardized testing can lead to some measures of accountability and a school's recognition of standards. And truthfully, if school leaders ignored such standards, it might lead to their job loss. But culturally responsive school leaders are explicit and honest about the benefit, or harm, that a focus on testing may have on the communities they serve. Testing has not been proven to help communities, and standardized tests have been harmful in many ways. But if the decision to emphasize testing is out of a principal's control, then there are indeed several decisions that are well within the control of school leaders. Choosing culturally responsive school staff is one of those decisions, as described next.

CULTURAL RESPONSIVENESS
AND SCHOOL SUPPORT STAFF

Joe was very strategic about hiring people who had a solid community presence and identity. In other words, he hired staff from multiple communities, even if they had not been taught or "trained" in how to interpret schooling in the same ways that educators had. For example, Mark, who has served as a community liaison and student mentor, was a former student who had been awarded a basketball scholarship; he was a towering presence at 6'8" and the students trusted, respected, and had a deep rapport with him. "Grandpa" was a long-time community presence who helped with the meals. Sheila, also a community liaison, had a close, intergenerational relationship with students and families. She was typically invited into homes, but even when she needed to contact a family and visit unannounced, she was not viewed with skepticism or suspicion. This was because her relationships with families were based on mutual respect, trust, credibility, and deep community-based rapport.

Such rapport was possible because the conversations and discourses between staff and parents were typically based on what was in the best interest of communities and students. Conversations were *not* based on test scores or other perceived schoolcentric challenges that students were facing. By hiring people from the students' communities, Joe did not merely want "people who looked like the students." Rather, the UAHS leader was fostering community-centric perspectives based on community histories. Below is a list of staff positions that must also receive training on cultural responsiveness. Also, leaders should consider hiring these staff persons from the Indigenous communities:

1. *Cultural/school-community liaisons.* **Why?** Although principals can develop structures that allow teachers to visit communities, liaisons are the only staff who will be constantly in the community and who can convey community-based perspectives to school staff. They can be true advocates for the community.

2. *Office staff.* **Why?** These are often the first people whom parents and students encounter. They have the power to be welcoming

and inclusive, or to be unhelpful, standoffish, or exclusive. Unfortunately, educators and principals typically do not know how some minoritized families may be treated by office staff, but the environment cultivated by these staff members can convey a powerful message to people within the community and school.

3. *Cafeteria staff, hall monitors, and bus drivers.* **Why?** Minoritized students are often disciplined before and after school, during lunchtime, on the bus, and between classes. And they use these spaces to interpret the overall school climate. These staff members, and others such as office, coaching, maintenance, and other staff, have rarely had training on cultural responsiveness, even if some teachers have had such training. Yet they have power and often significantly contribute to a culturally responsive school environment.

4. *Coaches/athletic staff.* **Why?** Coaching jobs are some of the most privileged and powerful positions in schools, but if coaches are not culturally responsive, they can also be the most marginalizing. While coaches yield a significant amount of influence on students, not much research has been done on whether coaching staffs have community-based people and perspectives in leadership positions.

5. *District staff.* **Why?** While district administrators cannot control the makeup of a school board, other positions at the district offices should include people who represent all segments of the community. District staffs are almost always policy implementers, and thus exercise immense policy influence (power) in a district. They must have community-based sensibilities when crafting/implementing policy, enrolling students, reporting information, and managing personnel issues.

6. *Equity team.* **Why?** Equity teams are a necessary component of culturally responsive schooling. They will lead in (a) crafting a

culturally responsive equity vision, (b) investigating equity issues, (c) monitoring progress, and (d) leading equity reforms. They have the role of establishing the community-based culture in a building, and in bringing along hesitant or skeptical colleagues. A culturally responsive equity team will be the driver for equity reforms in the school building, and its primary source of knowledge can be and often is community based.

FOSTERING A CULTURE OF CRSL AND ACADEMIC EXCELLENCE

The principal and leadership team are responsible for developing teacher capacity for creating culturally responsive curricula and pedagogy.[11] This capacity can be grown in multiple ways, including professional development in cultural responsiveness,[12] collaborative walkthroughs,[13] training teachers to use data to see gaps,[14] and mentoring and modeling CRSL behaviors for staff.[15] Also, it is absolutely imperative that CRSL principals are able to gauge teacher readiness for the capacity to change. By now, many educators may be thinking, "That's all good, but what's my bottom line? Does all of this have an impact on student learning?" The resounding answer is yes! A number of scholars have been able to demonstrate that culturally responsive leadership has a positive impact on student learning, self-esteem, academic success, and a sense of belonging in school.[16] Moreover, teachers feel a sense of empowerment and efficacy and thus perform better![17]

Yet, despite all of this evidence, we unfortunately hear that too many educators believe that terms such as *equity* or *culturally responsive* are synonymous with low or reduced expectations for students and their poor academic performance (see chapter 4). This belief is quite far from reality; in fact, scholars agree that culturally responsive work *must* maintain high expectations of students. Here are a number of strategies that culturally responsive school leaders can use to maintain both cultural responsiveness and high expectations of all students:

1. *Promote a vision of a culturally responsive, equitable, and inclusive school.* The very first task that CRSL principals and leadership teams must undertake is to craft and then promote a schoolwide vision of equity and excellence, inclusivity, and cultural responsiveness.[18] While principals and leadership teams may lead in setting the agenda, they should do so in close partnership with community-based voices, staff members, and students. The process of setting an initial vision can take up to a year, and thereafter will be ongoing. Leaders will continually need to check in with parents, teachers, and students to adjust the vision.

2. *Utilize equity teams as learning groups of practice.* I have visited hundreds of schools and districts, and every school has a different model for a school equity team. This is not necessarily bad, but there are some standard tasks this team must complete. As mentioned earlier, equity teams should collect relevant readings; lead professional development; collect, cohere/align, and interpret equity data; and build an inclusive culture based on the school's vision. In the context of this chapter, learning groups of practice and school equity teams are responsible for ensuring that curricula and pedagogies are culturally responsive. *Equity teams will need to have a representative from each subject area who can help to collect and research cultural knowledge and lessons that are relevant to the students' lives.* This will be an ongoing task, and therefore requires release time for team members to collect and disseminate relevant resources.

3. *Foster academic identity and high expectations.* On the first day I met Joe, I stayed with him all afternoon and into the evening.

On that day, he had kept two UAHS students at the school until 7:00 p.m. because they had not completed their homework. He and other staff rotated in staying after school hours to help students who could not (or chose not to) finish their homework the night before. Usually these were newer students, because the other students had already learned that it would be best to hand in homework on time. However, because of the close relationship Joe had with the community, this was not viewed as a hostile administrative act, but rather as an act of love: "He was doing this because he cared." But for the students and parents at UAHS, test scores really did not mean much. Therefore this was not something that Joe emphasized with them. For students and parents, it was important to improve their academic behaviors, have "good" grades (i.e., passing), and go to college after school. Whenever Joe asked which students had plans to go to college, *every* student would raise his or her hand.

4. *Reject low expectations, from deficitizing to deal making.* At UAHS, teachers exhibited low expectations of students in two ways. First, teachers attributed poor student performance to the community itself by describing the community with deficit characteristics. For example, Marvin, a Black social studies teacher, said that students do not do their homework because they have the immense responsibility of "taking care of their younger siblings after school because their parents are at work." But at every opportunity, Joe flatly rejected lowering expectations for students based on real or imagined community-based attributes. On two occasions, I heard him respond to similar teacher discourse by saying: "Don't tell me what they *cannot* do based on what happens in the community; tell me what they *can* do because of what happens in the community."

Second, a few UAHS teachers engaged in deal making with students, which is a tactic that lowers academic expectations for minoritized students. For example, teachers may offer to give students a certain letter grade in exchange for desired student behaviors. It sounded something like this: "If you sit in the corner and don't bother me or other students, I will give you a C." Or, "Go down [from science class] to the gym and work there for the remainder of this week." It is understandable that the teachers desired classroom harmony, but Joe rejected both of these teacher responses. In other school districts, I have also seen the "buddy room" and "buddy pass" practices, whereby teachers exchanged their challenging students. But more often than not, this served only as a disciplinary measure of control; no learning was associated with it.

5. *Be a warm demander.* Scholars have discussed how teachers should be "warm demanders"[19] for minoritized students, which "begins with establishing a caring relationship that convinces students that you believe in them."[20] I argue that principals must both take the lead in developing teachers who are warm demanders and maintain relationships directly with students. These relationships will allow leaders to encourage students to succeed academically in ways that students will interpret through the lenses of love and care. Students will believe that leaders are doing this *for* and not *against* them (i.e., that your high expectations are in their best interest). At UAHS, I noticed that staff genuinely cared for the students and their communities, which fostered strong school-community relationships.

I extend the notion of warm demanders to the relationships Joe had with UAHS students, teachers, and parents. It might be expected that he held a loving and caring relationship with students, and then leveraged this relationship to hold high expectations. But how did he do this with teachers or parents? The same way: he established a deep and caring relationship with them, and humbly asked for their help. *Parents* saw Joe ask for their perspectives and incorporate their feedback into school policy; he visited their homes and confirmed the humanity of their children. So when he asked to have their children in the summers and evenings for "additional help to bring them up to speed," they willingly complied. Similarly, *teachers* saw Joe emphasize the humanity of students and communities, and put time and resources into communities, and they too grew to trust him.

6. *Use community to influence teaching practice.* Throughout this book, I have shared examples of how one school leader used community-based knowledge and perceptions to craft school vision, enhance relationships, enrich curricula, promote an inclusive school vision, and humanize student identities, among other things. Yet, students will not learn from you if they do not like or trust you. So while curricula can be enriched, I also argue that teaching techniques must be informed by community-based knowledge and care.

At UAHS, teachers incorporated hip-hop into many subject areas, whether by having students examine the lyrics and grammar, explore the content (contained in songs), or discuss contexts (hip-hop as a response to oppressive contexts that early rappers faced). Scholars have widely published on the use of hip-hop in curricula, but what was striking at UAHS was how hip-hop was present in the language and mannerisms of teaching, or, for lack of a better term, the "swag" of how some UAHS teachers taught.

7. *Mentor teachers and support teacher modeling.* Before Joe began to directly challenge teachers who exhibited marginalizing behaviors, or who refused to incorporate culturally responsive teaching and pedagogies, he (and other successful teachers) would mentor teachers and model culturally responsive practice for them. At UAHS, Joe offered to provide mentoring for

teachers—both White and Black—who were unable to teach minoritized children. In much the same way that teachers are mentored when test scores reveal gaps in student learning, teachers should also receive mentoring when data shows that they have exclusionary teaching and disciplinary practices.

I noticed two circumstances in which Joe offered mentorship to teachers. In one circumstance, equity data indicated a teacher had racial equity issues around achievement and discipline. Second, Joe offered mentoring to teachers who tended to have behavior problems in their classes and seemed unable to "relate to the kids." For Joe, this meant that they needed more cultural training. In addition to mentoring, Joe modeled anti-oppressive and culturally responsive behaviors. He asked teachers who were inexperienced in cultural responsiveness to partner with and watch more experienced culturally responsive educators. The years of openly talking about equity and community had paid off in a big way—there was a culture of staff helping each other to become successful, and both the teacher mentors and mentees felt comfortable sharing ideas and learning from each other.

8. *Provide culturally responsive training and professional development.* Many schools across the United States bring popular trainers who host discussions about race, poverty, difference, or relationships. Few are able to shift the conversation to how culturally responsive schooling can become institutionalized and sustainable. Discussions about race are good, but fairly quickly, those conversations need to move into what system-level reforms must begin to occur to attain cultural responsiveness in all aspects of schooling. An obvious first step is an equity audit, but after that, school leaders must bring in scholars who understand research, and how research-based findings (that are reported in equity audits) can be linked to culturally responsive change.

When considering training, it is important to get both process and content experts. Districts and schools often make the mistake of getting only leadership reform experts (e.g., how to improve systemwide sustainable and equitable reforms) or subject-area experts (e.g., how to make science culturally responsive). But sustainable reform plans should entail both—that is, community people who can help add cultural knowledge as well as a CRSL person who can help improve structures that can embrace the deep cultural work.

"THAT'S THE PROBLEM! THE KIDS CAN'T SEE THEMSELVES IN THIS": FOSTERING CULTURALLY RESPONSIVE CONTENT

I use this final section to reemphasize a point made throughout this book. Culturally responsive principals are responsible for ensuring that the schools they lead are culturally responsive environments— classroom by classroom of course, but also in all other aspects of schooling. They have several ways of accomplishing this, and there are several components to achieving culturally responsive schooling. This chapter has dealt specifically with the role leaders can play in fostering culturally responsive teachers and curricula. For teachers to be able to recognize the cultural assets and capital that minoritized students possess, they must turn to the community; they cannot fully learn this cultural knowledge from books, university professors, or principals. Rather, teachers must humbly work with parents, students, and other community members to "unlearn" and then discover how to best serve their unique community. And principals must use their resources and power to enable community access.

For UAHS students to see themselves in classroom content and curricula, Joe encouraged teachers to get ideas from the community and directly from the students. A notable example during my time was how the technology teacher connected a lesson to a local hip-hop performance that included UAHS students. Joe had informed me about an upcoming hip-hop performance by a group with several UAHS students as members. He had already asked teachers to come out and show support to the students. The concert was held during a street fair outside of a youth nonprofit, located in a downtown space. I attended the concert, as did several UAHS teachers and locals who came to witness the music and concert.

Following the concert, Ray, the technology teacher, moved a lesson up and used the concert and a community-based event to enrich the content in a class. He presented a unit lesson on sound and acoustics, and connected it to how the students could have better sound quality during performances. The deep rhythmic bass sounds in the students' song were played on different types of speakers and were slowed down and sped up. Over the course of the week, Ray made a lesson around the dynamics of sound travel. And students seemed engaged as they connected with content that they recognized. Teachers who are committed to culturally responsive pedagogy can develop similar community-based subject-area lessons. The activities in figure 5.3 will help school leaders and educators check to see if the students feel connected to classroom curricula and content.

CONCLUSION

This chapter presents data on how principals can support teachers in becoming and remaining culturally responsive. Culturally responsive school leaders hire and develop teachers who will humanize students in their classrooms. In earlier chapters, I described humanization as a practice in which students' community-based identities are honored—that is, their cultural behaviors are identified and normalized by school staff—and leaders establish an inclusionary culture that accepts these students in school. Since many teachers are not able to recognize the cultural assets and perspectives of minoritized

FIGURE 5.3 Activity (45 days): Culturally responsive curriculum checks

1. While only an equity audit (incorporating student/community voice) can truly reveal whether or not a curriculum is culturally responsive, there are initial assessments that can be completed in school. Identify a representative group of forty minoritized students. (*Representative* means that all the different minoritized cultures and incomes must be represented at the meeting, as well as students who have different academic and disciplinary experiences.) Then, have the large group split into four grade-level groups (roughly ten students) and select research leaders. Next, contact a local Indigenous or minoritized researcher and ask that person to help empower the youth with Youth Participatory Action Research (YPAR) skills. And yes, you will have to pay this YPAR expert researcher to train the student researchers until your organization institutionalizes the skill. Have the student researchers conduct focus group interviews, and include the YPAR researcher and elders from the minoritized communities. Have the students, teachers, community elders, and YPAR expert collectively interpret the data. Here are some of the types of curriculum-related questions that students should ask their classmates in the focus group interviews:

   • Does the classroom content, like readings and class discussions, include examples from your community? Explain and give examples.
   • Have you ever felt connected with something you learned in class? Explain and give examples. Describe the last time you felt really connected to some content.
   • Have you ever felt disconnected from something you learned in class? Describe the last time you felt really offended by or disconnected from some content. Explain and give examples.
   • Do our classroom activities include things from your local community?
   • Does learning ever happen in your community? Explain and give examples.
   • Are individuals from your community ever involved in the learning activities, both in school and in the community? Explain and give examples.
   • Have teachers ever asked you or your parents about what types of things should be taught (or learning materials included) in class? Explain and give examples.
   • Do you feel comfortable telling the teacher about your interests? Explain and give examples.

2. Display all responses in an anonymous table. Did any common responses emerge from the student focus groups? Report out trends.

3. Come up with a recommendation for the principal about what curriculum changes should happen.

Principal's Task

This curriculum research project will require several types of leadership support: financial support for community-based participants and the YPAR expert, help in bringing the teams together, courage if some stakeholders begin

continues

FIGURE 5.3 *Continued*

> to push back against transferring curricular power to students and community
> voice, policy to ensure that the changes are not advisory but are binding, and
> checks to make sure that all minoritized groups are represented.
>
> **Superintendent's Task**
>
> The superintendent should institutionalize student-led research projects that
> are connected to curriculum and pedagogy, across the district. This not only
> values and centers student and community voice, but also connects these
> voices to power (i.e., the ways that curriculum, instruction, and pedagogy
> happen in the district).

students and parents, the principal's use (and honoring) of community knowledge and perspectives can make teachers better educators. Table 5.2 offers tips about how leaders can promote culturally responsive learning in schools.

Indeed, though some administrators promote culturally responsive culture, climate, and communities of practice, this chapter highlights how they must personally contribute to developing teachers and content. This fostering requires principals to provide opportunities for teachers to enter communities and learn from community members. It requires the direct hiring of people from the community, including those who are completely independent and who have not been trained to think like educators.

And finally, the student successes that followed were phenomenal. Nearly all UAHS students graduated, and the majority went on to study in postsecondary institutions. Suspensions were virtually nonexistent because, in addition to being humanized, the students reported that they liked learning at UAHS and that they trusted their teachers. In addition to his own deep relationship with UAHS students, Joe established the school conditions that led students to feel that all of the UAHS staff cared about them, their communities, and their success. So with their emotional/psychological safety intact, the UAHS students reported being academically engaged.

TABLE 5.2 Improving classroom instruction by engaging the community

CRSL curricula, instruction, and pedagogy	Traditional teacher role	Examples of CRSL instructional leadership behaviors
Lesson planning	Use in-school, online, and library resources to supplement the curriculum.	Establish a list of community members who can co-construct lessons with teachers.
Teaching a lesson	Use the book and curriculum provided by the district.	Provide opportunities for teachers to spend time in communities they serve, learn from community members, and then develop lessons that mirror community interests; coteach with elders.
Finding culturally responsive content	Purchase cultural books, use videos, or look online for supplemental materials.	*Example 1.* Obtain community-based newspapers, magazines, and publications to use in class. *Example 2.* Identify and pay community members to establish various learning programs in which they partner with teachers. *Example 3.* Identify issues of minoritization/oppression in the students' communities, and connect course content to advocating for those issues.
Classroom management	Write and post rules on the wall, call parents, send letters, and involve school leaders when students are not compliant.	Establish a community-based mentoring program with young mentors from students' neighborhoods.

But above all, I have tried to highlight the integral role that parents and other community members have in contributing to culturally responsive classrooms. I shared examples of how culturally responsive school leaders should rely on community-based knowledge and perspectives to inform teaching and curricula and to promote culturally responsive environments. This chapter shows that culturally responsive school leaders can provide training and professional development, mentor and model for teachers, and bring community knowledge and interests into the classroom.

CHAPTER 5

Discussion Questions

For Principals

1. Collect the forms or documents that are used in your school for the teaching or administrative tasks listed below. For each document, answer the following questions: How can you reframe this document with language that would make it more equitable and culturally responsive, and incorporate community-based voice and perspectives? What are some culturally responsive accountability measures you could incorporate in the next one to two years for each of these tasks?

- Lesson plans
- Administrative observations
- Administrative walk-throughs
- Job interviewing questions
- Staff meeting agenda formats
- Annual reviews for teachers
- School goals, objectives, and annual plans

2. What conditions are you looking for when partnering your culturally responsive teacher mentors with novice teachers (i.e., those who lack culturally responsive training/preparation)?

3. List ways that you can incorporate culturally responsive accountability measures within the next one to two years.

4. How can you find resources and time (PD days, for example) to enable teachers to spend time in communities learning and establishing trust, rapport, and credibility?

For Teacher Leaders

1. Make a list for each content area and come up with subject-specific sources of knowledge and resources from community that will allow for culturally responsive content.

2. Based on the teacher-specific data from the equity audit (or equity assessment), come up with one-year and two-year improvement plans for each teacher.

3. Meet with representative students and community members before the following task. Provide a list of the support you need from the building administrators, community members, and district-level administration to make this work possible. (These lists of support are only advisory and should not be used as an excuse to not engage the work!)

For Superintendents and District Office Staff

1. Draft a plan that would include community members (as paid members) in the district's goal/vision and instructional improvement plans.
2. Propose a way to introduce accountability measures around equity and school discipline. How will you accurately measure progress? Hold principals accountable?
3. How can you redirect PD dollars, title grant dollars, or funds from other sources to conduct an equity audit/equity assessment for your district? List concrete ways you will use this data to inform reforms.
4. Identify all district-level policies—from hiring policies, contract language and union negotiation protocol, and provisional teacher tenure policies to community engagement policies—and draft a plan to insert concrete measurable language around equity and cultural responsiveness. Draft a three-year plan, during which time all policies will be updated (don't forget to work on this with a member from the community!).

PROMOTING ANTI-OPPRESSIVE SCHOOLING THROUGH CULTURALLY RESPONSIVE SCHOOL LEADERSHIP
The Central Role of Community

Banishment from the homeland, the diaspora of a nation, the exile of a people, and ongoing colonization—these are the legacies Minnesotans and Americans have left to Dakota people. What do these legacies mean to the hearts and spirits of Dakota people? Most of us do not care to think too deeply about them, because the difficulties of everyday living as colonized peoples would be infinitely more difficult if we dwelt in a place of inconsolable grief.

—WAZIYATAWIN[1]

And maybe we need to leave the schools and go to the community.

—JOE

In her scholarship on the liberation of the Dakota, Waziyatawin's work compels me to consider a question: How can we reform education without understanding the realities of the people we serve? And why are social justice and transformative leadership models not enough for cultural responsiveness? It is not enough to want to fight for equity; school leaders must establish structures that will infuse all forms of leadership with unique community cultural knowledge, epistemology, and perceptions. I hope that the vivid ethnographic portraits here allow us to move past loose definitions and vague claims about culturally responsive school leadership. These narratives bring to life the theoretical and practitioner-based writings that predominate the field. And while I commend and honor our teacher-education colleagues for the work they have done with culturally relevant teaching, I am excited to be advancing the work on culturally responsive leadership. This book comes as we leadership scholars are still only at the beginning of our journey; others will certainly go above and beyond what is contained in this book.

In this final chapter, I summarize my data and findings and further theorize on the readings covered throughout the book. I argue that CRSL is not only necessary for critical self-reflection, but that it is the only way to attain schoolwide cultural responsiveness and equity-based reform. While culturally responsive teaching and policy implementation are important, they are simply not enough for comprehensive and sustainable culturally responsive schooling. In light of the provocative data in this book, I also argue that cultural responsiveness in schools will never be reached if leaders enact only traditional forms of leadership. Instructional leadership, transformational leadership, curriculum development, and professional development are all important school leadership functions, but they cannot continue to ignore the role that cultural responsiveness plays in each of these areas.

Traditional school leaders are often visible only within the school walls and at a few sporting events. This book pushes the role of the school leader deeper into the students' communities. This shift significantly expands traditional notions of school-community relationships: it not only requires a mutual presence, but also an engagement in and advocacy for community-based causes. Much of my earlier work and the work of other researchers all demonstrate how principals must regularly venture into communities, *on the community's own terms*.[2] Moreover, the nature of the relationship must begin with the community's interests (not test scores, grades, or student behavior) at the heart of the agenda. And last, principals' advocacy for issues important to the community is the secret ingredient that will eventually give principals the credibility, rapport, and trust that they so often long for. Throughout this book, I have presented glimpses of both community members being present in school, and of school staff being committed to and present in community spaces. In this conclusion, I make a strong case that principals can offer better leadership when they have a strong connection with and reliance on community-based people, perspectives, epistemologies, and voices.

EFFECTIVENESS OF CRSL

I contend that CRSL practices are effective in promoting culturally responsive and sustaining schools. But this effectiveness looks different depending on the goals. So, for example, when the CRSL goal was to improve pedagogical practices for minoritized students, I shared data indicating how UAHS students said they connected with the content and classroom learning. But when the CRSL goal was to promote a critically self-reflective staff and school (i.e., organization), the result was that UAHS teachers and leaders consistently searched for and confronted issues of oppression in their school. And when the CRSL goal was to foster inclusive school environments, UAHS students said that they felt a sense of belonging and safety in school. While not the focus of this book, more traditional effectiveness measures were also positive at UAHS. For example, the UAHS enrollment rate hovered around 95 percent, the graduate rate was over 90 percent, virtually all UAHS students professed that they had plans to attend college after graduation, and years passed without suspensions. While these traditional measures tell part of the UAHS story, table 6.1 summarizes the effective CRSL behaviors and related outcomes highlighted in this book.

TABLE 6.1 Summary of effective CRSL behaviors and outcomes

CRSL behavior	Examples of outcomes
Critical self-reflecting (chs. 1–2)	• Regular conversations occur about racial oppression. • Equity data helps to lead reforms. • Community voice informs practice.
Promoting inclusive environment (ch. 3)	• Teachers don't accommodate disengagement. • Students don't feel overpoliced and disciplined. • Suspension/expulsion rates decrease.
Humanizing student identities (ch. 4)	• Students can comfortably identify as smart. • Stereotypes are pronounced, and thus combatted. • All identities are welcomed in all school spaces.
Promoting culturally responsive curriculum and instruction (ch. 5)	• Lesson plans/content are culturally responsive. • Community plays an active role in pedagogy. • Test scores and grades for students improve.

ESTABLISHING COMMUNITY CREDIBILITY, RAPPORT, AND TRUST

Trust between schools and Black, Brown, Indigenous, and other minoritized communities has traditionally been low due to historical and current practices of marginalization. When I taught in Detroit Public Schools, many of the teachers spoke of parents with suspicion and mistrust. On the other hand, parents often mistrust the school as well. In this study, the case of one parent, Nikki, exemplified the mistrust between schools and community. Here is a sample from my field notes and a quote from Nikki:

My field notes: Nikki has two daughters at UAHS. Last year, one of her daughters went to UAHS but returned to her traditional school this year. Within months, [this daughter] felt marginalized again and began to fall behind. When Nikki herself tried to visit the traditional school her daughter had returned to, they made her sign in to the office and wait for thirty minutes in order for her to see her child in class. By that time, that period's bell was about to ring, and the parent just left frustrated. She then started sneaking in the back door of the traditional school to see her child in class, and then "signing in" as she exited the school. She explains:

> Joe tells you, "Come in, okay . . . anytime!" When I was at [the other schools], you gotta sign in, you need to call before you come. To me, if I need to call in before I come, you're hiding something, okay? You're hiding something and that was true over at [the middle school] or [the high school]. I always came into the school, but instead of signing in at the start of my visit, I would sign out, and secretly sign in when I left. I went through the back doors 'cause they would call a teacher up and say, "Miss [Henderson's] coming, here she come again." If my child is acting up and misbehaving to the point where you're gonna kick my child out, I wanna see her act up.

This statement from Nikki reveals a deep mistrust toward her daughter's traditional public school. Given schools' histories in contributing to the marginalization of certain communities, it is easy to see how minoritized communities may lack trust in their schools. Examples of marginalizing behaviors of districts, schools, and educators include these actions:

- Calling parents only when educators feel students are problematic
- Disciplining (i.e., shaming, referrals, suspensions, expulsions, court citations, arrests) minoritized students in disproportionate and oppressive ways
- Closing schools that are not profitable, even when they serve community needs
- Removing minoritized teachers and principals who are beloved by their communities (this has happened recently in communities such as New Orleans, but occurred across the country following the 1954 *Brown v. Board of Education* case)
- Disconnecting from/not caring about students' community life
- Using curriculum that does not represent students' lives

There are many behaviors like this that shape how communities view schools. But when, for example, Black students are suspended five or ten times more than White students (for the same offenses), it is hard for the Black community *not* to interpret this in light of community-based histories. This is precisely why I encourage schools to establish relationships that are not schoolcentric. Here are a few suggestions for school leaders to help improve their credibility, rapport, and trust with local communities:

1. Find out what is important to the community. Become involved with and advocate for these values even if they are not related to school. (Do not attempt to lead the effort; instead, follow the community.)

2. Use school resources to enable community members to have a constant presence in your school.

3. Use school resources to facilitate a nondisruptive presence of teachers and staff in the community.

4. Take an active antiracist and anti-oppressive stance, particularly on issues relevant to your students' community.

5. Be honest with students and families about how you (e.g., leaders, teachers, the school) have been complicit in oppression, and convey to them how you are trying to become better. Ask for their help.

6. Find ways to have a representative community voice; do not engage exclusively with the most vocal, visible, or engaged parents, or the most representative minoritized communities. This will take work and new strategies.

7. Publicly share your vision (in minoritized community spaces) for how you have listened to student and community perspectives, and how you have included these perspectives in school policy as well as classroom pedagogy and curricula.

SELF-DETERMINATION
AND COMMUNITY EMPOWERMENT

I realize that it may be controversial to suggest that we, as educators, should focus on community-based goals in addition to school-based goals. I have been criticized for not making student achievement the central goal for educators. However, I am not questioning the importance of student achievement, but rather how we get there! My central argument here is that by learning about and embracing community interests, and by humanizing students in school, educators *can* contribute to student achievement. How? Educators learn how to connect curricula and instruction with the lived experiences of students; they establish trusting relationships that are needed if students decide to stay and learn from them; they gain the support of community elders and learn what is important to them and their collective aspirations. Educators affirm student identity by having people from their communities in school. Educators and school leaders will then begin to be embraced by communities, and this rapport is grounded in trust. Hence, there is an added benefit of centering community-based perspectives in how we do schooling: we support the self-determination and empowerment of communities.

Scholars have identified ways that schools can be racist and that policy can be crafted so it continues to benefit only White interests and the schooling status quo. In the introduction and chapter 1, we learned that historical structures (i.e., leadership and policy) of oppression within and around schools persistently block educational opportunities for minoritized students and push them out of school. But we cannot *only* critique structures of oppression. I argue that educational leaders must pursue community-based goals that support communities' self-determination and community-based epistemologies; that is, leaders must consider how school policies and decisions will lead to a wholesome and dignified existence for the collective minoritized communities they serve. In this way, these communities can become self-sustaining and have a role in determining what is in their own best interests. Obviously, healthy communities are good for schools, and schools that contribute to better minoritized communities can support stronger students. The examples below show how both schools and communities benefit from having self-determinizing communities:

- *More Indigenous/minoritized teachers.* When schools are able to identify (and help develop) teaching talent within minoritized and Indigenous communities, they get the minoritized teachers they always claim to seek. But this also leads to job restoration and growth within the communities they serve. If you have not recruited teachers directly from tribal colleges, Hispanic-serving institutions, and historically black colleges and universities, do not claim that you cannot identify diverse teaching talent.
- *More Indigenous/minoritized role models.* The presence of minoritized role models can help to improve overall school climates. This also gives communities a chance to influence how schooling happens, which again can lead to job growth for minoritized students and communities. If you have not reached out to local community-based organizations, do not claim you cannot find minoritized mentors.
- *Community financial empowerment.* While it is clear how financial empowerment will benefit minoritized communities, did you know that when parents have a stable, good income, students perform better in schools? Researchers Chiu and Khoo found this to be the case not only in Western countries, but across the globe![3]
- *Healthier communities.* Researchers have firmly established two important findings pertaining to health and communities.

One, healthier students learn much better. And two, when communities are marginalized or oppressed, the students and communities get sicker. For example, it has been well documented that racism not only leads to depression and other mental illnesses, but actually causes physical illness.[4]

- *Protected communities.* Issues such as the *mass incarceration* of Black men, *deportations* of Latinx and South Asian immigrants, and *banning* Muslims from immigrating to the United States all contribute to a fearful hysteria in some communities. It is necessary that all community members—including those who seem not to be directly impacted—*feel safe.* When educators advocate for the protection and safety of communities, students can feel safer and thus learn better.

ORGANIZING A CULTURALLY RESPONSIVE SCHOOL: TWO INITIAL CHECKLISTS

Educational leaders should resist notions that they will ever create *completely* culturally responsive schools. Rather, they should think of this work as an iterative cycle of (a) constantly engaging in critical self-reflection and (b) implementing and/or reforming policies and practices that will make schools *more* culturally responsive. Here, I share two initial checklists that could help in this journey. These lists can be adjusted to meet your unique needs. First is a checklist of activities for the first three years of creating a culturally responsive school. Second, I list ways that school leaders can address common challenges faced in this work.

Checklist 1: Years 1–3 of Implementation

Listed on the following pages are key steps that should be taken to organize a culturally responsive school.

YEAR 1

- Complete a district (or school) equity audit that makes visible any inequities, identifies the sources of inequities, and connects the inequities to appropriate reforms.[5]
- After learning of the trends in your school/district, identify your role in contributing to the inequities (i.e., engage in critical self-reflection). Invite the community to partake in the conversation about these inequities.
- Identify policies that contribute to disciplinary or academic inequities in school.
- Identify practices that contribute to disciplinary or academic inequities in school.
- Establish systemwide (school or district) activities that cause critical self-reflection of all programs, departments, and practices.
- Identify equity partners in the building, invite them to join the work, give them the power to make binding changes, and enable them with the social capital and freedom to establish allyship (i.e., creating strategic alliances that work together toward equity and social justice) with other teachers.
  - Compose an equity team that is as representative of all school staff as possible. This includes leaders, teachers, support staff, office staff, parents, students, central district administrators, and others.
  - Establish a strong research component for both finding and conducting relevant research.
  - Get consensus on the role and responsibilities of the equity team.
- Establish an equity vision and common vocabulary for the school that highlights oppressive trends, equity, and cultural responsiveness.
- Examine how the local community has been marginalized over the years by the school and other official institutions (such as

judicial entities or law enforcement, social service organizations, under- or disinvestment by financial institutions, etc.); educate entire staff (including noninstructional staff) on this history.

- Allow teachers to spend four to six days per year in the communities they serve.
- Find spaces and times for parents and community members to have regular access to school facilities, and equitable input into policy making and reforms.
- Establish a five-year equity reform plan that will contribute to cultural responsiveness; have specific measurable one-year goals.
- Work with the union (or other legal stakeholders) to begin building a culture of accountability for equity data and cultural responsiveness that will be examined at the teacher level.

YEAR 2

- Complete an equity audit to monitor any changes in measures of equity in the building from year 1 to year 2.
- Institutionalize critical self-reflection activities.
- Institutionalize common language around cultural responsiveness, equity, and anti-oppressiveness.
- Identify diversity in community stakeholders (from across different communities and from within homogeneous communities); identify multiple ways of getting community voice, perspective, and epistemology at the center of school reform.
- Provide informational meetings on equity for the school board.
- Develop a protocol for hiring new staff that will be committed to cultural responsiveness.
- Look at school forms, tools, and documents and integrate equity components.
- Review roles and responsibilities of the equity team; ensure that schoolcentric perspectives are not muting community-centric perspectives.

- Establish a rotational method (how people will be transitioned on and off the team) and instructional method (ensuring that community-based ways of conveying knowledge are represented) of the equity team.
- Delegate a percentage of all regular meeting time to enhancing cultural responsiveness and equity.
- Begin building culturally responsive curricula and teaching techniques:
  - Begin to financially invest in and compile curricula resources.
  - Encourage at least one person from each curriculum team to join the equity team.
  - Establish mentoring and modeling structures that provide development for teachers who are struggling with cultural responsiveness.
- Have biannual critical self-reflection meetings; account for one-year goals.
- Begin to regularly discuss teacher-specific equity data.

YEAR 3

- Complete an equity audit to monitor any changes in measures of equity in the building from year 1 to year 3 and also from year 2 to year 3.
- Establish the capacity for school staff to continue conducting their own annual equity audit (without support from outside experts).
- Begin to establish a culture of equity accountability.
  - Have one-on-one meetings with teachers and staff members about their equity progress.
- Rotate equity team members (I suggest a two- or three-year term with 25 percent team turnover, but the rotational method should be one that makes sense for the school).

- Establish a community oversight committee of school decision making, which would review practices such as discipline, special education and gifted and talented referrals, grade retention, civic engagement, and so on (this should be primarily community-driven).
  - Rotate community oversight committees; choose a representative sample of the community members to represent the committee.

Checklist 2: Responses to Implementation Challenges

This checklist outlines ways that school leaders can address common challenges they may encounter as they promote culturally responsive school environments.

CHALLENGE: PUSHBACK FROM TEACHERS AND SCHOOL STAFF

Responses:

- Lead with data (perform equity audit).
- Invite staff to be part of the work.
- Push the agenda forward with staff who are supportive even without complete buy-in from all staff.
- Grow your team.
- Involve community members and students in discussion.
- In advance, develop and discuss responses to the most common types of emotional pushback: guilt, anger, denial, diversion, race-neutral talk, diversion to gender or socioeconomic status, and other ways that some staff may disengage from equity work.

CHALLENGE: PUSHBACK FROM THE SCHOOL BOARD OR COMMUNITY MEMBERS

Responses:

- Inform district administrators/superintendent of culturally responsive leadership vision.
- Enlist school board support.

- Invite school board members into community-led or student-led research projects.
- Discuss the histories of marginalization and oppression with school board members.
- Share current research that would help everyone contextualize the equity work.
- Develop and discuss responses to pushback in advance.

CHALLENGE: PUSHBACK FROM THE CENTRAL DISTRICT LEADERSHIP

Responses:

- Lead with data (perform equity audit).
- Share research-based scholarship.
- Partner with prominent allies in the community.
- Partner with students and parents.
- Discuss the histories of marginalization and oppression with school board members.
- Share current research that would help everyone contextualize the equity work.
- Develop and discuss responses to pushback in advance.

CHALLENGE: COSTS ASSOCIATED WITH DOING EQUITY WORK

Responses:

- Identify resources in Year 1 to confront financial challenges.
- Identify reforms not associated with costs, and begin there.
- Find other schools across the district that will partner in this work and share costs.
- Partner with community-based organizations and/or universities on projects that will improve cultural responsiveness and equity.
- Write for grant funding; approach local foundations to support the work.
- Incorporate cultural responsiveness and equity throughout all of the work that educators and leaders already do (but maintain designated days and times to discuss the work; both approaches are necessary).

PROPERLY HONORING
COMMUNITY-BASED EPISTEMOLOGY

Educators must be aware that they cannot "learn" community-based epistemologies. White teachers should not venture into Indigenous and minoritized communities to "learn about" the student. In other words, it is inappropriate to conduct research on communities. Research activities should be done with great care, and should be led by students, parents, and expert researchers. This is why I suggest that educators advocate for community-based goals: it gives educators a good reason and opportunity to enter and honor Indigenous community spaces. If teachers and principals do decide to venture into the community, they must do so in culturally appropriate ways. Here are just a few suggestions: (1) do not appropriate or attempt to lead the community's struggle, but feel free to support it; (2) decenter schoolcentric reforms; (3) give special reverence to the perspectives of community elders, but deeply honor the youth voices and views as well.

Does Everyone Deserve a "Redemptive Pathway"?

In a recent conversation with my colleague Dr. Peter Demerath (from the University of Minnesota), we discussed some of his racial equity work that happened in Falcon Heights, Minnesota—the city in which Philando Castile was killed by a police officer. After the shooting death of Philando Castile, the city of Falcon Heights established a racial justice commission that was supposed to lead conversations about how to reform policing, and racial bias therein. Dr. Demerath had some discomfort around one of the possible folks who was to also serve on the commission, and he discussed his discomfort with his colleague Kenneth Morris, a renowned attorney and expert. Morris responded to Dr. Demerath's discomfort by saying, "Peter, everyone deserves a 'redemptive pathway.'"

In my works in school districts across the United States, school leaders have held out a similar hope for all of their teachers: "But

Dr. Khalifa, I believe all of my teachers can change for the better." So the *education* "redemptive pathway" gives the opportunity for all teachers and staff to become "right," and to do better by their students; that is, to become more equitable and culturally responsive. I argue that we must believe in the redemptive pathway, and provide such a pathway to all educators. But I also believe that the lives of students and community members must be the deciding factor of when and how we reform schools. In other words, if after opening the redemptive pathway to a particular teacher to no avail—and after mentoring, and modeling, and having data-driven equity conversations about this person's practice and how his or her marginalizing practice is limiting the educational and life opportunities of, for example, Muskogee (Indigenous Native American) male students—the CRSL leader will eventually need to close the redemptive pathway and move in the best interest of students and communities.

"But My School Is Already All Black!": How to Respond

I often encounter educators and leaders in districts and schools that are predominantly minoritized. The conversations often follow a familiar course:

SCHOOL LEADER: But my school is already all Black; so how is this PD relevant to what we do?

MY RESPONSE: I am going to ask a series of questions, but please allow me to finish the questions before you respond because I suspect that you will have a single-word answer: Do you have non-Black teachers? And have *all* of your teachers received anti-oppressive and culturally responsive development? And is it not possible for types of oppression to occur on Black students attending a predominantly Black school? And if you feel the need to compare, can you not compare your

Black students with other students in nearby schools/ districts? And are you not aware that Black students who attend "all-Black schools" often live in communities that have experienced disinvestment, redlining, overpolicing, and so on?

SCHOOL LEADER: No.

MY RESPONSE: It is likely that your school may even need to engage this culturally responsive work more. And, unfortunately, it is also likely that your teachers may *think* they need it less. Thus, I suggest that you be even more intentional about community-based advocacy and outreach, for these students and communities can often be the most vulnerable.

SCHOOL LEADER: But I don't understand, Dr. Khalifa! What I'm saying to you is that we don't have an achievement gap. Our students are all Black!

MY RESPONSE: Should your school success be based on how closely Black students perform in comparison to White students? Or should you not aim for cultural responsiveness for your Black students, despite how they perform in comparison to White students? In other words, let's say for example that the suspension rates and academic achievement of your Black students are on par with nearby White students—does that automatically mean that they are not pressured to leave schools? Think of the dropout rate in your city as you answer that.

Does that mean that students are humanized, and that their self-determination and community-based aspirations are centered by your educators? Remember, culturally responsive schooling is about community engagement, relevant teaching and curriculum, and honoring students and their communities. All of this must be present in your school.

White Students as Reproductive Agents: How to Respond

I earlier mentioned that in one of the more recent equity audits, middle-school White students were espousing some White epistemology and racial bias that older Whites in the community were expressing. For example, some of the young White students were using deficit language to describe how the "new students" (i.e., migrant Latinx families who decided to stay because of jobs at meat-packing plants and other industry) brought problems into the district. Some of the White students were repeating, almost verbatim, some of the establishment White stereotypical discourses about Black students always being resistant and disobedient. CRSL leaders, and particularly White CRSL leaders, must confront this in their schools.

CRSL school leaders must understand that in the absence of culturally responsive work, even in all-White schools and spaces, White racial frames of White supremacy and White dominance can easily be passed on.[6] Just as there is a need for CRSL work in all-Black schools, so too do all-White schools—or spaces within diverse schools—need this work. Not only can they benefit from US Indigenous, Black, and Latinx epistemologies and frames, but they can become aware of their privilege, and become allies in CRSL work. Many White students will go on to have access to power and positions in society that minoritized students will never have. They must engage in these efforts every bit as much as teachers, leaders, and minoritized students and communities. In sum, it is not about whether or not White students will reproduce things like privilege, access, and power, but about where and for whom they will reproduce.

FINAL VIGNETTE: INTERGENERATIONAL, COMMUNITY-BASED (ANCESTRAL) KNOWLEDGE

I conclude chapter 6 and this book with a description of one of my final visits to the community where this study occurred. The Wilson family invited me into their home with Joe, who had a long history with the family. During the visit, Joe had a lively exchange with family members about the community's disposition toward "minority families," and about how the school "was on the side of the families." The conversation included a current UAHS female student (De'Janae), her mother (April), and grandmother (Helen)—all of whom had been Joe's students at the school. The mother and grandmother attended UAHS because they did not perform well in public schools, and because of their positive experiences and a sense of belonging at UAHS, they actually requested that De'Janae be sent to this school as well. The vignette illuminates Joe's presence in the community and the trust, rapport, and credibility that Joe had with those he served. Joe's support of community-based knowledge and experiences in school—what some scholars refer to as ancestral knowledge—helped him to understand the community and created community support for his school leadership. Below is an exchange between Joe, Helen and April. Occasionally De'Janae and her little brother De'ante add their thoughts:

JOE: When I got here, it was so bad for the Black families already here. They wanted to kick all of the Blacks and even Latinos out of the district. And when I came, I said, "I'm not having that!" And you've got to let me do what's in the best interest of these families, or I ain't coming.

HELEN: Yup. Because right around that time, Mike had gotten stabbed and Ron was murdered. So the schools just went crazy on us. They kicked me out and they have been doing that for the past thirty years.

JOE: Doing what?

HELEN: Trying to kick Black students out of the district at every opportunity they get. 'Cause when I had her [April] that was their excuse to try to get rid of me. But luckily you opened this school.

APRIL: Well, naw, it ain't only that. I didn't have her [De'Janae] until I left school, but they still kept pressuring me to leave the school too. It's like they hated seeing us but they had to deal with us. But UAHS was better for us—well, way better—because if we stayed at [the traditional high school] then it woulda been bad. I mean, even in the [traditional high school] they were always looking for ways to separate us out from the White students and I don't even know if they knew they were doing it.

JOE: Hell, they knew they were doing it because that's why they called me. But they also called on some of the other Black principals because some of them were part of the problem.

HELEN: Don't even go there! Some of them were worser than the White principals. It's like they had something to prove.

DE'JANAE: Yeah, the principal at [the public high school] was Black, but it's like he's not Black. I didn't like him, but all of the worse White teachers, like, really loved him.

JOE: But what do you think of our school? How could we make it better?

HELEN: Tell him the truth.

DE'JANAE: I like it; like, I can feel like I'm myself and don't have to always be stressed out and on edge. And they [the teachers] act like they care, and they want me there. Like, I ain't gonna lie, I don't like staying after school to finish my homework. But at [the public high school], I used to always be beefin' [at odds] with my teachers, but at UAHS I know y'all care about me so I don't mind y'all being a little harder on me.

DE'ANTE: Yeah, I'm gonna go there next year too. I hate my school now.

This exchange demonstrates the deep relationships that Joe had with those he served. But it also shows his insistence that the school was there to work for community interest and empowerment. Joe was not neutral in this regard; he was an advocate for issues and causes that community members themselves prioritized. This exchange also shows the power and effectiveness of CRSL for minoritized students' sense of belonging and academic success. In many schools, students choose to leave (dropout/pushout) because they face hostile climates and feel unwelcomed. The relationships that Joe had with students and families—which he invested in and encouraged his staff to have—actually changed the community's perception of this school. The students, who had previously been pressured out of the district's traditional schools, now identified as good students who wanted to go to college. Thus, when the positive, humanizing relationships were in place, UAHS students finished school more often, attained better grades, and went on to enroll in postsecondary learning institutions. And perhaps of equal importance, this vignette suggests that the narrative in the community—which informs how students view and engage with schools—had shifted. It now reverberated with what so many students said—"Joe and the teachers at UAHS actually care [about us, our families, our future]."

NEUTRALITY, COLONIZING LEADERSHIP, AND THE CONTINUED OPPRESSION OF OUR YOUTH

This passage between Joe and community members also demonstrates something that has to come to the forefront of school leadership discussions when it comes to serving communities. Communities already have histories and experiences that shape how they see schools. For minoritized communities, these experiences have often not been positive, and that explains why students and communities often mistrust schools and educators. The good news is that by interacting with communities in culturally responsive ways, school leaders can promote new ways for schools and educators to serve communities. This will lead to new ways that parents, students, and communities experience, and view, schools.

Can Blacks Be Racist? Why Systems Matter

Scholars have found that Indigenous, Black, and Latinx principals lead in different ways than White principals, and in ways that are impactful to both minoritized students and White students. The research is very powerful because it suggests that school districts must use resources to recruit and develop principals from minoritized groups. But it is also important to note that school districts that support the status quo will attempt to find minoritized individuals who will lead schools in ways that maintain current conditions. This chapter's vignette suggests that, while Black principals were hired to deal with problems of racism in the district, some of those Black principals instead reproduced systems of White supremacy and oppression. Others are the true embodiment of culturally responsive leaders. Thus, if there are racist practices in a district, it is necessary that all principals confront racism. *No leader*, despite his or her race, can have a pass on CRSL work. White supremacy, racism, and other systems of oppression will continue to be reproduced if principals are not explicitly anti-oppressive and culturally responsive. In fact, Christine Sleeter and other scholars have discussed necessary attitudinal beliefs of teachers who are committed to cultural responsiveness and educational equity.[7] In figure 6.1, I use Sleeter's work to suggest a number of necessary attitudinal traits of school leaders who hope to be culturally responsive.

CONCLUSION

School leaders must come to terms with the historical experiences of the communities they serve. For many minoritized communities,

FIGURE 6.1 Attitudinal traits of culturally responsive school leaders

- **Courage:** Is willing to make leadership decisions knowing that central district administrators, school boards, union officials, or building staff may not be happy.

- **Connectedness:** Feels connected to community-based causes.

- **Humility:** Constantly looks for signs that she or he is reproducing oppression in the school; will take that information head on, and institutionalize the appropriate anti-oppression reforms.

- **Deference:** Constantly looks for ways to lead with community, and use community-based and Indigenous knowledge to inform school policy and reform.

- **Intolerance:** Refuses to accommodate any forms of oppression in school.

- **Distributive:** Is always looking for ways to shift power and set the agenda for school policy and reform toward not just staff, but community.

- **Decolonizing:** Constantly seeks ways to (a) find, critique, and confront historical oppressive structures, and (b) build/promote structures that embrace community-based epistemologies, behaviors, and perceptions.

- **Humanizing:** Is able to reflect on his/her own aspirations, but is also aware that students and communities have their own Indigenous/ancestral knowledge and aspirations (desires, dreams, and goals apart from those of schools); leaders are willing to place these community-based aspirations at the center of the conversations around school pedagogy, curriculum, and leadership.

these have been histories of oppression and unrecognized agency; schools have often been a part of historically marginalizing those communities. And now many of you are leading those very same schools. What does that mean for your leadership practice? The research in this book and others like it suggest that your leadership must be explicitly and actively anti-oppressive. I have urged here that you seek to understand how you may be continuously contributing to oppression in your schools. Anti-oppressive leadership practices require us to lead schools in ways that confront and resist racism, colonization, and other types of oppression—we know much on how *not* to lead schools. But anti-oppressive leadership, alone, still leaves unanswered questions about how schools *should* actually be led. For that, I have turned to culturally responsive school leadership.

I have argued that culturally responsive principals have to institutionalize multiple practices, simultaneously. These are practices that many principals have likely *not* learned in their leadership preparation programs. Culturally responsive principals promote schooling practices that ask educators to engage in critical self-reflection and to constantly ask how they have been oppressive to students or communities. Culturally responsive principals also seek to understand—and encourage their teachers and staff to understand—the community's ancestral knowledge, experiences, and perceptions. Principals use this knowledge in multiple ways: to craft schools as a space inclusive of all students; to not only make school climates safe, but also to honor, humanize, and promote *all* student identities; and to build capacity to courageously move toward cultural responsiveness and institutionalize ways that educators use community-based and ancestral knowledge in their curricula and instruction.

But what about community? Community is central to my argument. Culturally responsive school leaders engage communities in nonexoticizing ways; they do not lead teachers in attempting to "train" or study communities; they do not reach out only with school-centric goals or negative news about students. Rather, they establish positive rapport and trusting relationships with communities; they use school resources to establish overlapping spaces wherein both school and community members are comfortable crossing those historical boundaries that have kept them apart; they use community epistemology and elders to craft and revise school policy for mentoring and for oversight of school practices; and perhaps most important, they resist the urge to be neutral or "official" as they enter communities and advocate for community-based goals. It is this way of leading schools in troubled times that will lead to both community empowerment and better schools.

NOTES

INTRODUCTION

1. I provide a detailed description of the term *minoritized* later, but for purposes here, it is a term that signals the active historical and current oppression that these students face. I use this word, instead of terms like *minority, students of color, underserved,* and so on, because these students did not simply choose to become "minority." They were made to be minorities, usually for economic, political, and racist reasons.

2. Thomas J. Sugrue, *The Origins of the Urban Crisis: Race and Inequality in Postwar Detroit* (Princeton, NJ: Princeton University Press, 2014). Sugrue's book and similar texts—such as Reynolds Farley's *Detroit Divided* (Reynolds Farley, Sheldon Danziger, and Harry J. Holzer, *Detroit Divided* [New York: Russell Sage Foundation, 2000]) and Detroit historian Richard Thomas's collective works, but in particular, Richard W. Thomas, *Life for Us Is What We Make It: Building Black Community in Detroit, 1915–1945* (Bloomington, IN: Indiana University Press, 1992)—would all later situate my students' context for me. But at the outset of my teaching, I was not aware. I argue that every teacher needs similar knowledge of contexts before they begin teaching in their areas.

3. Though the CIA denies involvement, this is accepted as truth in many US Black communities, and was represented in a number of documentary films, such as *Panthers: Vanguard of a Revolution,* and in major motion pictures such as *Kill the Messenger.*

4. Elizabeth T. Murakami et al., "Latina/o School Principals: Identity, Leadership and Advocacy," *International Journal of Leadership in Education* 19, no. 3 (2016): 280–99.

5. Vanessa Siddle Walker, *Hello Professor: A Black Principal and Professional Leadership in the Segregated South* (Chapel Hill, NC: University of North Carolina Press, 2009), 175.

6. Jerome E. Morris, "A Pillar of Strength: An African American School's Communal Bonds with Families and Community Since Brown," *Urban Education* 33, no. 5 (1999): 594.

7. For additional works, see Vanessa Siddle Walker, "Caswell County Training School, 1933–1969: Relationships Between Community and School," *Harvard Educational Review* 63, no. 2 (1993): 161–83; Vanessa Siddle Walker, "Organized Resistance and Black Educators' Quest for School Equality, 1878–1938," *Teachers College Record* 107, no. 3 (2005): 355–88; Vanessa Siddle Walker, "Valued Segregated

Schools for African American Children in the South, 1935–1969: A Review of Common Themes and Characteristics," *Review of Educational Research* 70, no. 3 (2000): 253–85.

8. Linda C. Tillman, "Chapter 4: African American Principals and the Legacy of Brown," *Review of Research in Education* 28, no. 1 (2004): 102.

9. Eva Gold et al., "Bringing Community Organizing into the School Reform Picture," *Nonprofit and Voluntary Sector Quarterly* 33, no. 3, suppl. (2004): 54S–76S.

10. C. Cooper, C. Riehl, and A. Hasan, "Leading and Learning with Diverse Families in Schools: Critical Epistemology Amid Communities of Practice," *Journal of School Leadership* 20, no. 6 (2011): 760.

11. Angela Valenzuela, *Subtractive Schooling: US-Mexican Youth and the Politics of Caring* (Albany, NY: SUNY Press, 2010); Sandra M. Gonzales, "Abuelita Epistemologies: Counteracting Subtractive Schools in American Education," *Journal of Latinos and Education* 14, no. 1 (2015): 40–54; George F. Madaus and Marguerite Clarke, "The Adverse Impact of High Stakes Testing on Minority Students: Evidence from 100 Years of Test Data" in *Raising Standards or Raising Barriers? Inequality and High Stakes Testing in Public Education,* ed. G. Orfield and M. Kornhaber (New York: The Century Foundation, 2001).

12. Evelyn Nakano Glenn, "Settler Colonialism as Structure: A Framework for Comparative Studies of US Race and Gender Formation," *Sociology of Race and Ethnicity* 1, no. 1 (2015): 57.

13. William Watkins, *The White Architects of Black Education* (New York: Teachers College Press, 2001), 26–27.

14. For more information on this, see Na'ilah Suad Nasir, "'Halal-ing' the Child: Reframing Identities of Resistance in an Urban Muslim School," *Harvard Educational Review* 74, no. 2 (2004): 153–74; Na'ilah Suad Nasir and Jasiyah Al-Amin, "Creating Identity-Safe Spaces on College Campuses for Muslim Students," *Change: The Magazine of Higher Learning* 38, no. 2 (2006): 22–27; Loukia K. Sarroub, *All American Yemeni Girls: Being Muslim in a Public School* (Philadelphia: University of Pennsylvania Press, 2005); Tricia Seifert, "Understanding Christian Privilege: Managing the Tensions of Spiritual Plurality," *About Campus* 12, no. 2 (2007): 10–17; Muhammad Khalifa, "Validating Social and Cultural Capital of Hyperghettoized At-Risk Students," *Education and Urban Society* 42, no. 5 (2010): 620–46; Muhammad Khalifa et al., "Racism? Administrative and Community Perspectives in Data-Driven Decision Making: Systemic Perspectives Versus Technical-Rational Perspectives," *Urban Education* 49, no. 2 (2014): 147–81.

15. Jaideep Singh, "The Racialization of Minoritized Religious Identity: Constructing Sacred Sites at the Intersection of White and Christian Supremacy," in *Revealing the Sacred in Asian and Pacific America*, ed. Paul R. Spickard and Jane Naomi Iwamura (New York: Routledge, 2003): 87.

16. Khalifa, "Validating Social and Cultural Capital"; Suad Nasir, "'Halal-ing' the Child"; Sarroub, *All American Yemeni Girls*.

17. *Equity audits* are systematic ways of investigating and pinpointing the exact source of achievement and disciplinary gaps in school. It's not enough for districts to know that they have achievement gaps—they must also know why. The equity audit most closely aligned with this text can be done online at ajusted.org. Many equity audits focus on trends and disparities, and while ajusted.org audits do identify and describe disparities, they offer much more: surveys designed not only for teachers and administrators, but that also capture the student and parent/community voice. They also investigate the negative impact that district and school-based policies may be having on minoritized students.

18. See Ann Arnett Ferguson, *Bad Boys: Public Schools in the Making of Black Masculinity* (Ann Arbor: University of Michigan Press, 2001); Adam R. Jeffers, "Reflections of Academic Experiences from Formerly Incarcerated African American Males," *Equity & Excellence in Education* 50, no. 2 (2017): 222–40; Adam R. Jeffers, "Early Academic Experiences of Recently Incarcerated African American Males" (PhD diss., University of Southern California, 2010); Nathern Okilwa, Muhammad Khalifa, and Felecia Briscoe, eds., *The School to Prison Pipeline: The Role of Culture and Discipline in School*, vol. 4. (Bingley, UK: Emerald Publishing Limited, 2017); Russell Skiba et al., "Consistent Removal: Contributions of School Discipline to the School-Prison Pipeline" (paper presented at School to Prison Pipeline Conference, Boston, MA, May 16–17, 2003.

19. Nelda Cambron-McCabe and Martha M. McCarthy, "Educating School Leaders for Social Justice," *Educational Policy* 19, no. 1 (2005): 201–22; D. Pounder, U. Reitzug, and M. D. Young, "Preparing School Leaders for School Improvement, Social Justice, and Community," in *The Educational Leadership Challenge: Redefining Leadership for the 21st Century, Yearbook of the National Society for the Study of Education* 101, no. 1 (2002): 261–88; Muhammad Khalifa, "A Re-new-ed Paradigm in Successful Urban School Leadership: Principal as Community Leader," *Educational Administration Quarterly* 48, no. 3 (2012): 424–67; Lorri J. Santamaría, "Critical Change for the Greater Good: Multicultural Perceptions in Educational Leadership Toward Social Justice and Equity," *Educational Administration Quarterly* 50, no. 3 (2014): 347–91.

20. Judith L. Touré, "'There's Some Good Karma Up in Here': A Case Study of White School Leadership in an Urban Context" (PhD diss., University of Pittsburgh, 2008), 200.

21. Ira E. Bogotch, "Educational Leadership and Social Justice: Practice into Theory," *Journal of School Leadership* 12, no. 2 (2000): 138–56; Kathleen M. Brown, "Social Justice Education for Preservice Leaders: Evaluating Transformative Learning Strategies," *Equity & Excellence in Education* 38, no. 2 (2005): 155–67; Muhammad Khalifa, "Promoting Our Students: Examining the Role of School Leadership in the Self-Advocacy of At-Risk Students," *Journal of School Leadership* 23, no. 5 (2013); Murtadha, Khaula, and Daud Malik Watts, "Linking the Struggle for Education and Social Justice: Historical Perspectives of African American Leadership in Schools,"

Educational Administration Quarterly 41, no. 4 (2005): 591–608; George Theoharis, "Social Justice Educational Leaders and Resistance: Toward a Theory of Social Justice Leadership," *Educational Administration Quarterly* 43, no. 2 (2007): 221–58.

22. Lewis Madhlangobe and Stephen P. Gordon, "Culturally Responsive Leadership in a Diverse School: A Case Study of a High School Leader," *NASSP Bulletin* 96, no. 3 (2012): 177–202.

23. Mark A. Gooden and Michael Dantley, "Centering Race in a Framework for Leadership Preparation," *Journal of Research on Leadership Education* 7, no. 2 (2012): 237–53.

24. Walker, *Hello Professor*; Gerardo Lopez, "The Value of Hard Work: Lessons on Parent Involvement from an (Im)migrant Household," *Harvard Educational Review* 71, no. 3 (2001): 416–38; Kofi Lomotey, *African-American Principals: School Leadership and Success*, Contributions in Afro-American and African Studies, No. 124 (Westport, CT: Greenwood Press, 1989).

25. Gooden and Dantley, "Centering Race in a Framework for Leadership Preparation"; Colleen A. Capper, George Theoharis, and James Sebastian, "Toward a Framework for Preparing Leaders for Social Justice," *Journal of Educational Administration* 44, no. 3 (2006): 209–24.

26. Akhil Gupta and James Ferguson, "Beyond 'Culture': Space, Identity, and the Politics of Difference," *Cultural Anthropology* 7, no. 1 (1992): 6–23; Arjun Appadurai, ed., *The Social Life of Things: Commodities in Cultural Perspective* (Cambridge, UK: Cambridge University Press, 1988); Arjun Appadurai, "Putting Hierarchy in Its Place," *Cultural Anthropology* 3, no. 1 (1988): 36–49; George Jerry Sefa Dei, *Reconstructing "Dropout": A Critical Ethnography of the Dynamics of Black Students' Disengagement from School* (Toronto: University of Toronto Press, 1997); Michel Foucault, "The Body of the Condemned," in *The Foucault Reader*, ed. Paul Rabinow (New York: Pantheon, 1984), 171–78; Renato Rosaldo, "Cultural Citizenship, Inequality, and Multiculturalism," in *Latino Cultural Citizenship: Claiming Identity, Space, and Rights,* ed. William V. Flores and Rina Benmayor (Boston: Beacon Press, 1997).

27. Mehan, Hugh, Lea Hubbard, and Irene Villanueva, "Forming Academic Identities: Accommodation Without Assimilation Among Involuntary Minorities," *Anthropology and Education Quarterly* 25 (1994): 91–117; Khalifa, "Validating Social and Cultural Capital."

28. Nilda Flores-González, "Puerto Rican High Achievers: An Example of Ethnic and Academic Identity Compatibility," *Anthropology & Education Quarterly* 30, no. 3 (1999): 343–62.

29. Linda C. Tillman, "Mentoring New Teachers: Implications for Leadership Practice in an Urban School," *Educational Administration Quarterly* 41, no. 4 (2005): 609–29; Muhammad Khalifa, "Teacher Expectations and Principal Behavior: Responding to Teacher Acquiescence," *Urban Review* 43, no. 5 (2011): 702–27; Siddle Walker, "Caswell County Training School, 1933–1969," and *Hello Professor*; Kim Allen, Steve Jacobson, and Kofi Lomotey, "African American Women in Educational

Administration: The Importance of Mentors and Sponsors," *Journal of Negro Education* (1995): 409–22.

30. Chezare A. Warren, "Empathy, Teacher Dispositions, and Preparation for Culturally Responsive Pedagogy," *Journal of Teacher Education*, June 2017.

31. Khalifa, "A Re-new-ed Paradigm in Successful Urban School Leadership"; Morris, "A Pillar of Strength"; Siddle Walker, *Hello Professor*; Camille Wilson Cooper, "Performing Cultural Work in Demographically Changing Schools: Implications for Expanding Transformative Leadership Frameworks," *Educational Administration Quarterly* 45, no. 5 (2009): 694–724.

CHAPTER 1

1. Eve Tuck and K. Wayne Yang, "Decolonization Is Not a Metaphor," *Decolonization: Indigeneity, Education and Society* 1, no. 1 (2012).

2. Vanessa Siddle Walker, *Hello Professor: A Black Principal and Professional Leadership in the Segregated South* (Chapel Hill, NC: University of North Carolina, 2009. There have been significant advances in the cultural area of scholarship. See, for example: Terrance L. Green, "Leading for Urban School Reform and Community Development," *Educational Administration Quarterly* 51, no. 5 (2015): 679–711; Gerardo R. Lopez, Jay D. Scribner, and Kanya Mahitivanichcha, "Redefining Parental Involvement: Lessons from High-Performing Migrant-Impacted Schools," *American Educational Research Journal* 38, no. 2 (2001): 253–88; Camille Wilson Cooper, "Performing Cultural Work in Demographically Changing Schools: Implications for Expanding Transformative Leadership Frameworks," *Educational Administration Quarterly* 45, no. 5 (2009): 694–724; Muhammad Khalifa, "A Re-new-ed Paradigm in Successful Urban School Leadership: Principal as Community Leader," *Educational Administration Quarterly* 48, no. 3 (2012): 424–67; Mark A. Gooden, "The Role of an African American Principal in an Urban Information Technology High School," *Educational Administration Quarterly* 41, no. 4 (2005): 630–50; Kofi Lomotey, *African-American Principals: School Leadership and Success*, Contributions in Afro-American and African Studies, No. 124 (Westport, CT: Greenwood Press, 1989).

3. Muhammad Khalifa et al., "Racism? Administrative and Community Perspectives in Data-Driven Decision Making: Systemic Perspectives Versus Technical-Rational Perspectives," *Urban Education* 49, no. 2 (2014): 147–81.

4. Siddle Walker, *Hello Professor*.

5. Colleen L. Larson, "Is the Land of Oz an Alien Nation? A Sociopolitical Study of School Community Conflict," *Educational Administration Quarterly* 33, no. 3 (1997): 334.

6. Harold W. Pfautz, Harry C. Huguley, and John W. McClain, "Changes in Reputed Black Community Leadership, 1962–72: A Case Study," *Social Forces* 53, no. 3 (1975): 466.

7. Khalifa et al., "Racism?"; Larson, *Is the Land of Oz an Alien Nation?*

8. Muhammad Khalifa, forthcoming 2018.

9. See, for example: Michael L. Cooper, *Indian School: Teaching the White Man's Way* (Wilmington, MA: Clarion Books, 1999); Patrick Wolfe, "Settler Colonialism and the Elimination of the Native," *Journal of Genocide Research* 8, no. 4 (2006): 387–409.

10. Joshua Bornstein, "Can PBIS Build Justice Rather Than Merely Restore Order?" in *The School to Prison Pipeline: The Role of Culture and Discipline in School*, ed. Nathern Okilwa, Muhammad Khalifa, and Felecia Briscoe (Bingley, UK: Emerald Publishing Limited, 2017), 135–67.

11. Muhammad Khalifa, Mark Anthony Gooden, and James Earl Davis, "Culturally Responsive School Leadership: A Synthesis of the Literature," *Review of Educational Research* 86, no. 4 (2016): 1272–311.

12. Tracy Carpenter-Aeby and Victor G. Aeby, "Family-School-Community Interventions for Chronically Disruptive Students: An Evaluation of Outcomes in an Alternative School," *School Community Journal* 11, no. 2 (2001): 75–92; also see Vanessa Siddle Walker's collective works.

13. For example, see: Khalifa, "A Re-new-ed Paradigm in Successful Urban School Leadership"; Muhammad Khalifa, "Teacher Expectations and Principal Behavior: Responding to Teacher Acquiescence," *Urban Review* 43, no. 5 (2011): 702–27; Khalifa, Gooden, and Davis, "Culturally Responsive School Leadership; Muhammad Khalifa, "Can Blacks Be Racists? Black-on-Black Principal Abuse in an Urban School Setting," *International Journal of Qualitative Studies in Education* 28, no. 2 (2015): 259–82; Muhammad Khalifa, Noelle Witherspoon Arnold, and Whitney Newcomb, "Understand and Advocate for Communities First," *Phi Delta Kappan* 96, no. 7 (2015): 20–25.

CHAPTER 2

1. Africa Information Service, ed., *Return to the Source: Selected Speeches of Amilcar Cabral* (New York: Monthly Review Press, 1973), 166–68.

2. Muhammad Khalifa, Mark Anthony Gooden, and James Earl Davis, "Culturally Responsive School Leadership: A Synthesis of the Literature," *Review of Educational Research* 86, no. 4 (2016): 10.

3. Mark A. Gooden and Michael Dantley, "Centering Race in a Framework for Leadership Preparation," *Journal of Research on Leadership Education* 7, no. 2 (2012): 237–53; Colleen A. Capper, George Theoharis, and James Sebastian, "Toward a Framework for Preparing Leaders for Social Justice," *Journal of Educational Administration* 44, no. 3 (2006): 209–24.

4. Kathleen M. Brown, "Leadership for Social Justice and Equity: Evaluating a Transformative Framework and Andragogy," *Educational Administration Quarterly* 42, no. 5 (2006): 700–45; Michael E. Dantley, "African American Spirituality and Cornel West's Notions of Prophetic Pragmatism: Restructuring Educational Leadership in American Urban Schools," *Educational Administration Quarterly* 41, no. 4 (2005):

651–74; Michelle D. Young and Julie Laible, "White Racism, Antiracism, and School Leadership Preparation," *Journal of School Leadership* 10, no. 5 (2000): 374–415.

5. Khalifa, Gooden, and Davis, "Culturally Responsive School Leadership."

6. Several models of equity audit and assessment systems are available. I have tried to combine multiple models in one that I helped develop, called Ajusted™ Equity Audits (www.ajusted.org). This model looks at critical questions of equity and oppression, and recommends equitable reforms based on the data in the schools or districts that complete the audit; the cost per student is quite minimal because data collection does not require expensive researcher presence in schools; data is collected online instead.

7. George Lipsitz, *The Possessive Investment in Whiteness: How White People Profit from Identity Politics* (Philadelphia: Temple University Press, 2006).

CHAPTER 3

1. Susan Roberta Katz, "Presumed Guilty: How Schools Criminalize Latino Youth," *Social Justice* 24, no. 4 (70) (1997): 81.

2. Akhil Gupta and James Ferguson, "Beyond 'Culture': Space, Identity, and the Politics of Difference," *Cultural Anthropology* 7, no. 1 (1992): 8.

3. Ibid; Arjun Appadurai, ed., *The Social Life of Things: Commodities in Cultural Perspective* (Cambridge, UK: Cambridge University Press, 1988); Arjun Appadurai, "Putting Hierarchy in Its Place," *Cultural Anthropology* 3, no. 1 (1988): 36–49; George Jerry Sefa Dei et al., *Reconstructing "Drop-out": A Critical Ethnography of the Dynamics of Black Students' Disengagement from School* (Toronto: University of Toronto Press, 1997); Michel Foucault, "The Body of the Condemned," in *The Foucault Reader*, ed. Paul Rabinow (New York: Pantheon, 1984): 171–78; Renato Rosaldo, "Cultural Citizenship, Inequality, and Multiculturalism," in *Latino Cultural Citizenship: Claiming Identity, Space, and Rights*, ed. William V. Flores and Rina Benmayor (Boston: Beacon Press, 1998).

4. Ted N. Okey and Philip A. Cusick, "Dropping Out: Another Side of the Story," *Educational Administration Quarterly* 31, no. 2 (1995): 244–67; Dei et al., *Reconstructing "Drop-out."*

5. Bree Picower, "The Unexamined Whiteness of Teaching: How White Teachers Maintain and Enact Dominant Racial Ideologies," *Race Ethnicity and Education* 12, no. 2 (2009): 197–215; R. P. Solomon et al., "The Discourse of Denial: How White Teacher Candidates Construct Race, Racism and 'White Privilege,'" *Race Ethnicity and Education* 8, no. 2 (2005): 147–69.

6. Kathleen J. Martin and James J. Garrett, "Teaching and Learning with Traditional Indigenous Knowledge in the Tall Grass Plains," *Canadian Journal of Native Studies* 30, no. 2 (2010): 289.

7. For example, see Christopher Dunbar Jr., "African American Males and Participation: Promising Inclusion, Practicing Exclusion," *Theory into Practice* 38, no. 4 (1999): 241–46.

8. Frank Brown, "African Americans and School Leadership: An Introduction," *Educational Administration Quarterly* 41, no. 4 (2005): 587.

9. Kofi Lomotey, *African-American Principals: School Leadership and Success*, Contributions in Afro-American and African Studies, No. 124 (Westport, CT: Greenwood Press, 1989), 145–46.

10. Muhammad Khalifa, "Teacher Expectations and Principal Behavior: Responding to Teacher Acquiescence," *Urban Review* 43, no. 5 (2011): 702–27.

11. Okey and Cusick, "Dropping Out."

12. For a deeper level of analysis, see these and similar works: Glen Aikenhead, "Integrating Western and Aboriginal Sciences: Cross-Cultural Science Teaching," *Research in Science Education* 31, no. 3 (2001): 337–55; Eric Gutstein et al., "Culturally Relevant Mathematics Teaching in a Mexican American Context," *Journal for Research in Mathematics Education* 28, no. 6 (1997): 709–37.

13. Eva Wells Chunn, "Sorting Black Students for Success and Failure: The Inequality of Ability Grouping and Tracking," *Urban League Review* 11 (1988): 104.

14. Robert K. Ream, "Counterfeit Social Capital and Mexican-American Underachievement," *Educational Evaluation and Policy Analysis* 25, no. 3 (2003): 237–62.

15. Ibid.; Sharon Feiman-Nemser and Robert E. Floden, "The Cultures of Teaching. Occasional Paper No. 74" (East Lansing, MI: Michigan State University, Institute for Research on Teaching, 1984).

16. For earlier research that reports similar findings, see Michael W. Sedlak et al., *Selling Students Short: Classroom Bargains and Academic Reform in the American High School*. (New York: Teachers College Press, 1986).

17. See Lisa Delpit, *Other People's Children: Cultural Conflict in the Classroom* (New York: The New Press, 2006); Greg Wiggan, "Race, School Achievement, and Educational Inequality: Toward a Student-Based Inquiry Perspective," *Review of Educational Research* 77, no. 3 (2007): 310–33.

18. Linda C. Tillman, "Mentoring African American Faculty in Predominantly White Institutions," *Research in Higher Education* 42, no. 3 (2001): 295–325.

19. Nelda Cambron-McCabe and Martha M. McCarthy, "Educating School Leaders for Social Justice," *Educational Policy* 19, no. 1 (2005): 201–22.

20. For example, see Patricia Phillips, "A Self-Advocacy Plan for High School Students with Learning Disabilities: A Comparative Case Study Analysis of Students', Teachers', and Parents' Perceptions of Program Effects," *Journal of Learning Disabilities* 23, no. 8 (1990): 466–71; Deborah J. Merchant and Anna Gajar, "A Review of the Literature on Self-Advocacy Components in Transition Programs for Students with Learning Disabilities," *Journal of Vocational Rehabilitation* 8, no. 3 (1997): 223–31.

21. In addition to Siddle Walker's works, see Eva Gold et al., "Bringing Community Organizing into the School Reform Picture," *Nonprofit and Voluntary Sector Quarterly* 33, no. 3, suppl. (2004): 54S–76S.

CHAPTER 4

1. James Baldwin, "A Talk to Teachers," *Yearbook of the National Society for the Study of Education* 107, no. 2 (2008): 16–18.

2. Hugh Mehan, Lea Hubbard, and Irene Villanueva, "Forming Academic Identities: Accommodation Without Assimilation Among Involuntary Minorities," *Anthropology and Education Quarterly* 25 (1994): 91–117; Muhammad Khalifa, "Validating Social and Cultural Capital of Hyperghettoized At-Risk Students," *Education and Urban Society* 42, no. 5 (2010): 620–46.

3. Norma González, Luis C. Moll, and Cathy Amanti, eds., *Funds of Knowledge: Theorizing Practices in Households, Communities, and Classrooms* (New York: Routledge, 2006), ix–x.

4. Lisa Delpit, *Other People's Children: Cultural Conflict in the Classroom* (New York: The New Press, 2006), 25.

5. Ancestral knowledge can be briefly defined as community or people-based knowledge that is mainly oral but can be written, is intergenerational and thus passed down through family and community in unique ways, and carries information not only about "traditions," but about virtually every aspect of life. But because ancestral knowledge is often not written and is thus seen as illegitimate, unverifiable cultural knowledge, it has been exoticized or kept out of traditional schools.

6. Christine E. Sleeter, "Equity and Race-Visible Urban School Reform," in *Handbook of Urban Educational Leadership*, ed. Muhammad Khalifa et al. (Lanham, MD: Rowman & Littlefield, 2015), 135.

7. Khalifa, "Validating Social and Cultural Capital."

8. Stephen L. Morgan and Aage B. Sørensen, "Parental Networks, Social Closure, and Mathematics Learning: A Test of Coleman's Social Capital Explanation of School Effects," *American Sociological Review* 64, no. 5 (1999): 661–81.

9. Robert Palmer and Marybeth Gasman, "'It Takes a Village to Raise a Child': The Role of Social Capital in Promoting Academic Success for African American Men at a Black College," *Journal of College Student Development* 49, no. 1 (2008): 52–70.

10. Janice E. Hale, *Black Children: Their Roots, Culture, and Learning Styles* (Baltimore: Johns Hopkins University Press, 1982); Shawn A. Ginwright, *Black in School: Afrocentric Reform, Urban Youth and the Promise of Hip-Hop Culture* (New York: Teachers College Press, 2004); Theresa Perry, Claude Steele, and Asa G. Hilliard, *Young, Gifted, and Black: Promoting High Achievement Among African-American Students* (Boston: Beacon Press, 2003); Jeffrey M. Duncan-Andrade and Ernest Morrell, *The Art of Critical Pedagogy: Possibilities for Moving from Theory to Practice in Urban Schools* (New York: Peter Lang, 2008).

11. González, Moll, and Amanti, *Funds of Knowledge*, ix–x.

12. Nilda Flores-González, "Puerto Rican High Achievers: An Example of Ethnic and Academic Identity Compatibility," *Anthropology & Education Quarterly* 30, no. 3 (1999): 343–62.

13. Ramon Grosfoguel and Eric Mielants, "The Long-Durée Entanglement Between Islamophobia and Racism in the Modern/Colonial Capitalist/Patriarchal World-System: An introduction," *Human Architecture* 5, no. 1 (2006): 1; Walter Mignolo, *Local Histories/Global Designs: Coloniality, Subaltern Knowledges, and Border Thinking* (Princeton, NJ: Princeton University Press, 2012).

14. Tara J. Yosso, "Whose Culture Has Capital? A Critical Race Theory Discussion of Community Cultural Wealth," *Race Ethnicity and Education* 8, no. 1 (2005): 69–91.

CHAPTER 5

1. Karen Seashore Louis and Moosung Lee, "Teachers' Capacity for Organizational Learning: The Effects of School Culture and Context," *School Effectiveness and School Improvement* 27, no. 4 (2016): 534–56; Valerie E. Lee and Susanna Loeb, "School Size in Chicago Elementary Schools: Effects on Teachers' Attitudes and Students' Achievement," *American Educational Research Journal* 37, no. 1 (2000): 3–31; Valerie E. Lee and Julia B. Smith, "Collective Responsibility for Learning and Its Effects on Gains in Achievement for Early Secondary School Students," *American Journal of Education* 104, no. 2 (1996): 103–47.

2. Sonia Nieto, *The Light in Their Eyes: Creating Multicultural Learning Communities* (New York: Teachers College Press, 2015); Geneva Gay, *Culturally Responsive Teaching: Theory, Research, and Practice* (New York: Teachers College Press, 2010).

3. Louise Stoll and Karen Seashore Louis, *Professional Learning Communities: Divergence, Depth and Dilemmas* (Maidenhead, UK: McGraw-Hill Education, 2007).

4. Ibid., 2.

5. Ibid., 3.

6. Richard DuFour, "What Is a 'Professional Learning Community'?," *Educational Leadership* 61, no. 8 (2004): 6–11.

7. This came by way of a personal communication with Dr. Emily Palmer, who has published research on the topic. See Emily Lilja Palmer, "Talking About Race: Overcoming Fear in the Process of Change" (PhD diss., University of Minnesota, 2013); and Emily Lilja Palmer and Karen Seashore Louis, "Talking About Race: Overcoming Fear in the Process of Change," *Journal of School Leadership* 27, no. 4. (2017): 581.

8. To learn about the prospects of your district or school performing an equity audit, visit ajusted.org.

9. Muhammad Khalifa, Mark Anthony Gooden, and James Earl Davis, "Culturally Responsive School Leadership: A Synthesis of the Literature," *Review of Educational Research* 86, no. 4 (2016): 1272–311.

10. Charlotte Danielson, *Enhancing Professional Practice: A Framework for Teaching*, 2nd ed. (Alexandria, VA: ASCD, 2007).

11. Ana Maria Villegas and Tamara Lucas, *Educating Culturally Responsive Teachers: A Coherent Approach* (Albany, NY: SUNY Press, 2002; Margery B. Ginsberg and Raymond J. Wlodkowski, *Creating Highly Motivating Classrooms for All Students: A Schoolwide Approach to Powerful Teaching with Diverse Learners,* Jossey-Bass Education Series

(San Francisco: Jossey-Bass, 2000); Deborah L. Voltz, Nettye Brazil, and Renee Scott, "Professional Development for Culturally Responsive Instruction: A Promising Practice for Addressing the Disproportionate Representation of Students of Color in Special Education," *Teacher Education and Special Education* 26, no. 1 (2003): 63–73.

12. Ginsberg and Wlodkowski, *Creating Highly Motivating Classrooms for All Students*; Voltz, Brazil, and Scott, "Professional Development for Culturally Responsive Instruction."

13. Lewis Madhlangobe and Stephen P. Gordon, "Culturally Responsive Leadership in a Diverse School: A Case Study of a High School Leader," *NASSp Bulletin* 96, no. 3 (2012): 177–202.

14. Linda Skrla et al., "Equity Audits: A Practical Leadership Tool for Developing Equitable and Excellent Schools," *Educational Administration Quarterly* 40, no. 1 (2004): 133–61.

15. Muhammad Khalifa, "Teacher Expectations and Principal Behavior: Responding to Teacher Acquiescence," *Urban Review* 43, no. 5 (2011): 702–27; Linda C. Tillman, "Mentoring New Teachers: Implications for Leadership Practice in an Urban School," *Educational Administration Quarterly* 41, no. 4 (2005): 609–29.

16. Muhammad Khalifa, "A Re-new-ed Paradigm in Successful Urban School Leadership: Principal as Community Leader," *Educational Administration Quarterly* 48, no. 3 (2012): 424–67; Lorri J. Santamaria, "Culturally Responsive Differentiated Instruction: Narrowing Gaps Between Best Pedagogical Practices Benefiting All Learners," *Teachers College Record* 111, no. 1 (2009): 214–47.

17. Adrienne Alton-Lee, "Quality Teaching for Diverse Students in Schooling: Best Evidence Synthesis," *Building Teacher Quality, Research Conference 2003 Proceedings* (Camberwell, Australia: ACER, 2003), 24.

18. Mary E. Gardiner and Ernestine K. Enomoto, "Urban School Principals and Their Role as Multicultural Leaders," *Urban Education* 41, no. 6 (2006): 560–84; Lauri Johnson, "Culturally Responsive Leadership for Community Empowerment," in *Multicultural Education in Glocal Perspectives*, ed. Y.-K. Cha et al. (Singapore: Springer Singapore, 2017), 183–99; G. Webb-Johnson and N. Carter, "Culturally Responsive Urban School Leadership: Partnering to Improve Outcomes for African American Learners," *National Journal of Urban Education and Practice* 1, no. 1 (2007): 77–99.

19. Jacqueline J. Irvine and J. W. Fraser, "Warm Demanders," *Education Week* 17, no. 35 (1998): 56–57.

20. Elizabeth Bondy and Dorene D. Ross, "The Teacher as Warm Demander," *Educational Leadership* 66, no. 1 (2008): 54–58.

CHAPTER 6

1. Waziyatawin, "What Does Justice Look Like? The Struggle for Liberation in Dakota Homeland" (St. Paul, MN: Living Justice Press, 2008): 17.

2. For my earlier work, see Muhammad Khalifa, "A Re-new-ed Paradigm in Successful Urban School Leadership: Principal as Community Leader," *Educational*

Administration Quarterly 48, no. 3 (2012): 424–67; Muhammad Khalifa, No-elle Witherspoon Arnold, and Whitney Newcomb, "Understand and Advocate for Communities First," *Phi Delta Kappan* 96, no. 7 (2015): 20–25; Muhammad Khal-ifa, Mark Anthony Gooden, and James Earl Davis, "Culturally Responsive School Leadership: A Synthesis of the Literature," *Review of Educational Research* 86, no. 4 (2016): 1272–311.

See the works of others such as Camille Wilson Cooper, "Performing Cultural Work in Demographically Changing Schools: Implications for Expanding Trans-formative Leadership Frameworks," *Educational Administration Quarterly* 45, no. 5 (2009): 694–724; Terrance L. Green, "Leading for Urban School Reform and Community Development," *Educational Administration Quarterly* 51, no. 5 (2015): 679–711; Ann Ishimaru, "From Heroes to Organizers: Principals and Education Or-ganizing in Urban School Reform," *Educational Administration Quarterly* 49, no. 1 (2013): 3–51; Jerome E. Morris, "A Pillar of Strength: An African American School's Communal Bonds with Families and Community Since Brown," *Urban Education* 33, no. 5 (1999): 584–605; Vanessa Siddle Walker, *Hello Professor: A Black Principal and Professional Leadership in the Segregated South* (Chapel Hill: University of North Carolina Press, 2009).

3. M. M. Chiu and L. Khoo, "Effects of Resources, Inequality, and Privilege Bias on Achievement: Country, School, and Student Level Analyses," *American Educa-tional Research Journal* 42 no. 4 (2005): 575–603.

4. Camara Jules P. Harrell et al., "Multiple Pathways Linking Racism to Health Outcomes," *Du Bois Review: Social Science Research on Race* 8, no. 1 (2011): 143–57; Martie L. Skinner et al., "Allostasis Model Facilitates Understanding Race Differ-ences in the Diurnal Cortisol Rhythm," *Development and Psychopathology* 23, no. 4 (2011): 1167–86; David R. Williams and Selina A. Mohammed, "Racism and Health I: Pathways and Scientific Evidence," *American Behavioral Scientist* 57, no. 8 (2013): 1152–73.

5. I recommend the website ajusted.org, but there are plenty of other equity as-sessment tools available.

6. For more on this, see Timothy Lensmire's collective works, in particular his book: Timothy J. Lensmire, *White Folks: Race and Identity in Rural America* (New York: Routledge, 2017).

7. Christine E. Sleeter, "Resisting Racial Awareness: How Teachers Understand the Social Order from Their Racial, Gender, and Social Class Locations," *Journal of Educational Foundations* 6, no. 2 (1992): 7. Also see, for example, Belinda Bus-tos Flores and Howard L. Smith, "Teachers' Characteristics and Attitudinal Be-liefs About Linguistic and Cultural Diversity," *Bilingual Research Journal* 31, no. 1–2 (2009): 323–58.

ACKNOWLEDGMENTS

While this book presents my recent scholarship, it is equally a product of my experiences with educators across the country, my own professional experiences as a teacher and administrator in Detroit, my work in multiple international spaces, and critical conversations with my scholar friends.

I start by honoring the memory of my dear friend Joe Dulin (1935–2014). I spent more than two years with Joe. We traversed multiple spaces together—official and personal, community and school—and without the access he granted me, this book project would not have been possible. He touched many of our lives, and I will donate part of the proceeds of this book to the Joe and Yvonne Dulin Scholarship Fund.

My mother served as my first schoolteacher, and my father was the principal of the same private school in Detroit. Both my parents went on to become and to retire as educators in the Detroit Public Schools. My mom, Faith, and dad, Aziz, "grew" my interest in education. And many of my "uncles" and "aunts" from my Detroit community helped me along the way. Here, I name only a few of the many from whom I pull my strength: Dr. Abdulalim Shabazz, Nadir Ahmed, and Badriyyah Sabree. Khidhir Naeem, who also served as my placement teacher when I was a student teacher in Detroit, and Sherman Jackson, my spiritual mentor and just my guy, have pushed my thinking and helped me grow.

As I became a Detroit educator myself on the East Side, two people in particular saved my career. The first I'd like to thank is Mrs. Green. I was a first-year, very insecure teacher who felt the need to prove that I could take control of my class. I was yelling at the top of my lungs, but my students were still louder. Mrs. Green walked by and saw me struggling, and offered, "Baby, that's not how we do it here, but if you want me to, I can show you." She did. My next-door (classroom) neighbor, Dwight Nettles, was also a reliable mentor and friend during my teaching years in Detroit.

I also acknowledge and thank many academic mentors over the years who influenced my thinking about this work. It was actually quite strange for me to encounter such a familiar and loving group of scholars. It reminded me of the unconditional love that I experienced in my earlier years in Black Detroit. I could not understand why other professors were so loving and embracing toward me—a person they did not know. Though I only called him to ask a few questions, Christopher Dunbar recruited me into the doctoral program and would eventually go on to direct my dissertation. He is my greatest academic mentor and friend. When I was named a Barbara Jackson scholar, I attended a UCEA (University Council for Educational Administration) conference and met Linda Tillman, who immediately embraced me and told the other folks: "Go ahead, introduce yourself to him." It was that familiar love, and she had initiated me into a community. Then, James Davis agreed to mentor me for two years, and I've never allowed him to leave that role.

Until the last year in my doctoral program, I was planning to become the superintendent of Detroit Public Schools! When I suddenly decided to shift to an academic career trajectory for which I had not prepared, and all of my potential job leads fell apart, it was my loving friend and mentor Judy Alston who took a chance on me. My many conversations with my biggest academic mentor, Mark Gooden, have deeply shaped the scholar I have become. Thanks, homie. So many other scholars have offered friendship, guidance, and just kind, thoughtful words that have put my own scholarship on track and my anxieties at ease: Mike Jennings, Reitu Mabokela,

Gerardo Lopez, Khaula Murtadha, Kofi Lomotey, George Theoharis, Floyd Beachum, Betty Merchant, Camille Wilson, and Rodney Hopson. Special thanks to Felecia Briscoe and Noelle Witherspoon Arnold, with whom I have collaborated on multiple projects: you have shaped my thinking, enriched my soul, and given me hope.

Several Minnesota colleagues, most of whom are currently serving as educational leaders, commented on this work. Thank you to Katie Pekel, Emily Elijah Palmer, Joel Lear, and Ty Thompson for reading and commenting on portions of this book. I also appreciate my academic colleagues Peter Demerath and Karen Seashore for lending their mentorship and scholarly insights to this work.

I want to thank Lisa Delpit, my sister and friend. I have appreciated your kindness and guidance over the years, and I stand in perpetual appreciation for your foreword for this book. I also wish to acknowledge and thank Rich Milner and Douglas Clayton, and later Jayne Fargnoli, who served as editors; thank you for believing in this project from the very beginning.

Finally, yet most importantly, I appreciate my family, who have really borne the brunt of my long nights, early mornings, and constant time away as I completed this book. I could not have finished it without the support of my best friend and love, Nimo Abdi. My boys, Ibrahim, Adam, and Zack, teach me so much. I am so fortunate to have them as sons.

ABOUT THE AUTHOR

Muhammad Khalifa is the Robert H. Beck Professor of Ideas in Education in the Department of Organizational Leadership, Policy and Development in the College of Education and Human Development at the University of Minnesota. He has worked as a public school teacher and administrator in Detroit. He is most noted for helping districts perform equity audits as a way to address injustice and dehumanization in school, and has helped leaders select appropriate reforms that counter inequitable practices in school (www.ajusted.org). His research examines how urban school leaders enact culturally responsive leadership practices. He is coeditor of three other books: *Handbook on Urban Educational Leadership*, *Becoming Critical: The Emergence of Social Justice Scholars*, and *The School to Prison Pipeline: The Role of Culture and Discipline in School*. He has also published widely, with articles appearing in such journals as *Review of Educational Research*, *Teachers College Record*, *QSE*, *Urban Review*, *EAQ*, *Journal of Negro Education*, and the *Journal of School Leadership*. Dr. Khalifa has also contributed in Asian and African educational contexts, and most recently was invited to several post-conflict areas to improve education.

INDEX